MW01601359

This memoir is a truthful recollection of actual events and experiences in the author's life. Some dialogue has been recreated and some events have been compressed. The names and identifying characteristics of some individuals have been changed to protect and respect their privacy.

ISBN-13: 9798327789531

Cover design by: Canva Creative Studio

Library of Congress Control Number: 2018675309

Printed in the United States of America

Dedication

This book is dedicated to my beloved and supportive wife, Diona, with whom I have shared 16 years of marriage. Her encouragement has been the driving force behind the creation of this book, alongside our three beautiful children: Kai, Jordan, and Chase. As they progress through their educational journeys, it is my hope that the American educational system will evolve towards greater transparency, prioritizing future-focused education over being driven solely by standardized testing and financial motives.

Furthermore, I extend this dedication to every educator within the Moncur, Scavella, Stokes, Campbell, McKinney-Williamson, and the Historic Saint Agnes' Episcopal Church families. Moreover, this book is a tribute to all the students I have had the privilege to teach over the years. A special acknowledgment is extended to the remarkable individuals from my 2022-2023 Cambridge AICE U.S. History AS Level class, these young ladies shown unwavering support, inspiration, and embody the potential to become influential leaders in their own

right: Ki' Ani B, Trudean C., Doniella C., Megan D., DeJaya H.,

Amena H., Ar'Mani I., Herly J., Makayla J-L., and Michelle R.

Lastly, this book is dedicated to the memory of former

students who tragically lost their lives prematurely to gun

violence, suicide, and other devastating circumstances.

Table of Contents

Foreword

Over the years of working together at our school, I've come to see the author not only as a colleague but as a true advocate for change and a deeply passionate educator. His book, *"The Mis-Education of Today's Black Youth: Life in the Classroom"*, sparks an essential conversation for those of us dedicated to educational reform, particularly in schools predominantly serving Black students. It echoes Carter G. Woodson's insight: "If you can control a man's thinking you do not have to worry about his action."

We've shared over a decade of challenges and successes, giving me a close-up view of the real-life stories he shares in this book. These aren't just academic theories; they are the day-to-day realities we live, filled with moments both trying and triumphant. The author's route into teaching reflects a familiar story for many of us in this profession. Like so many educators, including myself, his entry into the classroom wasn't planned from the start; it was shaped by family traditions and the deep, rewarding aspects of teaching that have a way of pulling you in. His deep commitment to addressing the specific needs and opportunities for our Black students highlights a critical need for dedicated advocacy and tailored educational approaches. These aim to overcome not just systemic flaws but also cultural oversights. The stories he shares of our students' challenges and the practical difficulties we face every day underscore the urgent need for real, tangible solutions. Moreover, the author's background as a Morehouse College graduate adds a rich layer to his narrative, blending academic excellence and leadership into his teaching and now, into this enlightening book.

As you delve into this book, consider the wider implications of what we've learned together. The experiences outlined here reflect not just our local context but a nationwide imperative. This isn't just about critiquing; it's a call to action for everyone involved in education to help build a system that truly uplifts every student, preparing them for life, not just exams. Moncur's insights provide not just a critique, but a call to action for all stakeholders in education to strive for a system that uplifts every student, and prepares them for more than just academic tests, but for life's many tests.

Here's to moving forward! Let's embrace this opportunity for change and strive for an educational environment that truly honors and supports all students, particularly those who have long been marginalized. We, the dedicated black teachers of America, want more, much more for our black schools, our black families, our black teachers, and most importantly, our black students. Do you?

Renee O'Connor

Fellow Black Educator

African American History and

Cambridge AICE Global Perspectives and Research

Foreword

As descendants of people who were forced into involuntary migration and slavery from the motherland of Africa. We continue to desire change especially when it comes to education. The basic right to quality education must be fulfilled. During our formative years, our parents teach us that education is the great equalizer which would eventually level the playing field. However, what is perceived as education today will have you wondering and questioning what truly is happening in the classroom. Education has been watered down and commercialized to the point that the basic right and foundations to a quality education has been lost. What can be done to ensure that this issue is corrected and provide a degree of excellence in the classroom that students are entitled to, desired and need to become successful, productive citizens of society.

The Mis-Education of Today's Black Youth: Life in the Classroom is a profound and essential recollection through the eyes of a teacher in the actual trenches. Lemuel R. Moncur, who is a young black male, draws on his own experiences from being a social studies teacher in an urban high school classroom. He provides an authentic and modern interpretation of the issues and problems that teachers tackle in today's classroom such as lack of parental involvement, unrealistic expectations, and lack of support from administration, social media and the loss of learning impacted from the two years of home learning due to COVID-19. This book hopefully will lead to change in the educational system for students, especially black students; and serve as an eye-opener for educators and parents.

Maureen E. Campbell, Ph.D.

Retired Educator

Preface

When growing up, I never envisioned myself being an educator. I had other dreams and ideas of what I wanted to do when I grew up. Dreams and ideas that included being a pilot or working with computers. Even as I have gotten older, the thought of becoming a priest still comes to mind thanks to the late Father Richard L.M. Barry, the late Father J. Kenneth Major, Father Terrance Taylor, and Father Horace Ward from the Diocese of Southeast Florida of the Episcopal Church. But when your grandmother was an elementary school teacher for 25 years, your auntie is still teaching physical education, and a host of family members who have taught or are still teaching—it would be a matter of time before I followed this calling into education too. I began my educational career as a substitute teacher in January 2006, as it afforded me the opportunities to work at many different schools and it taught me that education is not always the top priority in every school. As a substitute, you truly understand how each school and administration operate differently, and plus you learn what is classroom management too.

The groundwork for writing this book is not being done out of spite, but rather seeing that there needed to be an advocate for our Black youths in today's school system. Having now been an educator with nearly 20 years in the classroom; more can be done to educate our Black youths especially for life's journey after high school. The traditional model in today's schools simply does not afford the success and accountability that our Black students need. Yes, I am fully aware that it's not all the school's fault, parents and students themselves must share the responsibility too. As an educator in a high school classroom, I noticed the significant decline in academic skills and capabilities of students as early as the 2016-2017 school year when I began teaching the Cambridge AICE U.S. History to students.

The true inspiration for this book occurred on Thursday, December 6, 2018, that day served as the official wake-up call for me to write this book and express my concerns. On that day in both my 6th and 8th periods, it confirmed everything for me about what is wrong with our educational system within our Black schools. I had students doing a mini practice for the Paper Two component for their Cambridge History exam that May

2019. On the Promethean Board, I had a write-up telling the students what their paragraph answers should include. During my 6th period, I had a student who exactly asked, *"What are we doing? Why do we have to write so much?"* I literally had to take a step back and start questioning my existence, my drive, and my passion for teaching this Cambridge curriculum. Is it time for me to leave this school and be like LeBron James *"and take my talents elsewhere"* to teach this course I asked myself? I did my best to explain in multiple ways, but *DAMN*! How many more ways can I decipher this to students who have low reading scores and simply cannot comprehend what I am asking them to write, or have the critical thinking skills? The other inspiration came during 8th period, where I had 15 students who have the drive to want to do well and even put their best foot forward to try and pass this exam. The problem is that there are another 15 students in the room. There is absolutely no way I can read each student's response. I am only but one person. It literally takes me 10 minutes before I can give the first student back their paper with feedback, because other students want me to read their papers or help with a question. How can it be done and what is wrong with this picture? That is what I am attempting to answer

with this book. I am hopeful that I can address these issues and

hopefully give solutions and insight into correcting them.

Although this book's original inspiration is six years past, those

same issues are still today's issues in 2024.

Lemuel R. Moncur

Introduction

Where are the Black youths of today going to be decades from now with little to no education? A question that many people have tried to answer, as well as other essential concerns. This book will try to answer these fundamental questions. However, it is important to remember that I cannot provide concrete answers to everything that is wrong in educating our Black youths in today's society. As I stated in the preface, this book is not written in spite, but to honestly bring attention to these matters and to have these conversations. I feel as though a lot of people know what the problems are, but no one really wants to talk about it openly without retaliation. The groundwork will be laid for further discussions to take place between parents, students, teachers and administration. A solid foundation of core literacy skills that are reading and writing needs to be an essential priority for students' learning. Education is important regardless of one's socioeconomic status, but Black schools must be afforded the same resources as their White counterparts. Black students' education must be valued straightforwardly with a strong emphasis to not succumb to standardized testing practices that are inherently racist and use student data from testing that is manipulated, and the lack of parental support and respect. Parents must be willing to step up and take ownership of the role they play. They must hold their child accountable for academic failures and behavioral issues as well, and not continue to enable or be a hindrance in defending these actions in the classroom. As the African proverb states, *"it takes a village to raise a child"*, everyone must be involved equally.

But it's also important in my opinion that we must stop pushing this philosophical idea that college or university is for everyone. ***College is not for everybody.*** Yes, every student who wants to go to college should be able to go, but we must stop pushing this idea on students who really have no interest. High schools should unquestionably offer two academic tracks for students: **(1)** college/university or **(2)** trade school. Therefore, giving them choices and options to either attend technical or vocational schools, the military or the workforce instead of attending a two-year or four-year college, and then racking up student debt with no degree to show for it. In my eight years of teaching seniors, I have seen too many of them who are neither college bound or have no plans after high school and are therefore ill-prepared for the real world. A cycle that must be broken for our Black students to become successful and financially stable and independent. Financial literacy courses must be readily available for high schoolers especially for seniors. Too many students today do not understand how credit works and its impact, debts and loans, savings and investments, and different insurances that they must manage throughout life. As I have shared with students before, no matter how successful you are, your credit will still be a determining factor. However, students are more concerned about passing scores on state assessments or having ACT/SAT concordant scores in order to receive their high school diploma instead of mastering literacy skills and just learning life skills. Where are the priorities of the states, local school districts, school administrators, and parents? Unfortunately, most students in this generation are more concerned with having their heads buried into their cell phones on social media, making TikTok videos in hallways and restroom stalls, and honestly believe in instant gratification which is a false narrative to begin with. There is still so much work ahead to level the playing field in education, but we all must work together as a village to accomplish these goals and aspirations.

Therefore, this book gives an intimate firsthand point-of-view from being a teacher in a Black urban high school classroom.

Chapter 1

There is this misunderstanding in education that many of our Black youth cannot learn or cannot be taught for multiple reasons. There is no doubt that technology and especially the use of cell phones today have been very detrimental to their learning capabilities. In order to have a transparent look at all these reasons, there will be numerous comments and inputs from not only my personal experience, but from current educators, students, and from my podcast [*Ray Talks Live*] for reference as to what is wrong with educating Black students in today's school system throughout this book. This chapter will address three issues which are the inept ability of teacher programs, those who are decision-makers with little to no educational experience, and inferior teachers in the classroom. These three issues can have long-term damaging effects in educating our Black youth today.

The first issue would be the Teach for America (TFA) program. Teach for America began as the undergraduate thesis of Wendy Kopp while at Princeton University. It was a program that began in 1990 with the intent that its corps would be widely used in underperforming schools across the United States.

Today, Teach For America receives hundreds of millions of public and private dollars and has garnered acclaim for sending college graduates, who do not typically have an educational background, to teach in low-income rural and urban schools for a two-year commitment. (Heilig & Jez, 2014)   Many school districts utilize the Teach for America program as a major asset mainly because most districts do not have to pay salaries in full; the district pays a percentage and TFA pays the remainder. So therefore, most districts encourage principals to hire TFA teachers for the classroom. From my own personal experiences in two high schools, TFA teachers were butting jokes and at times were detrimental to the education of Black students. Although Teach for America's website will state otherwise, there is a disconnect from what they are trained, to what they will actually experience in the classroom in low-income neighborhood schools. A firsthand example was when two new TFA teachers were hired in the social studies department for the 2016-2017 school year, one stated that his training was in Oklahoma, and that what he learned and experienced in five weeks was nowhere compared to what he was experiencing now.

"This approach differs from the traditional teacher education programs by condensing corps members' student teaching experience, lessons on core teaching concepts, and specialized training, while students in traditional teacher education programs typically spend a year or more building their skills through these activities and working alongside expert teachers." (Heilig & Jez, 2014)   Therefore many TFA teachers are ill-prepared and ill-equipped to **(1)** teach and understand that most inner-city Black youths are not on their grade level for reading and math. So the assignments given and expectations of teachers are not on par for where they should be. **(2)** Numerous TFA teachers are also unable to understand or relate to the issues and socioeconomic status of their students. An educator must be able to relate to their students to understand why they perform and/or act out a certain way in the classroom. Many TFA teachers are raised in middle- to upper-class households, graduating from some of the finest colleges and universities in the United States, and live a life that is in no way comparable to their students. How could they possibly understand the "inner-city kids" or the "hood life" where living on food stamps, neighborhood shootings, and drug and gang activities are the norms of their students' everyday life? **(3)** Most importantly, a multitude of TFA teachers are not in the program to serve its true purpose, most are in the program for the student loan forgiveness where they complete two to three years, and then simply leave the educational field at the first opportunity for their true career. Sarah Craig (2022) states "Corps members only teach for two years before they become alumni of the program, and oftentimes move out of the educational field entirely. The inconsistency created by TFA's two-year structures leaves students without opportunities to build long-term relationships with teachers, which can be crucial for marginalized students who already face systemic educational inequities". In other words, most Teach for America teachers are not in the program to truly teach our Black students, but simply to play "teacher" and then jump ship. Therefore, doing more damage to Black students than having a first-year teacher who went to undergrad as an education major surrounded by mentors. A suggestion by Levy (2011) states that "people work as paralegals before deciding to go to law school, why not have TFA candidates work as teachers' aides and then fund their further education if they pledge to go on to teach in high-poverty schools?" Jeff Bryant (2015) further adds that "Evidence of TFA's academic benefits to students continues to be a mixed picture at best, varying considerably depending on the experience and certification level of the teachers being considered. The results also fluctuate depending on the types of teachers to whom the TFA teachers are compared. TFA teachers look relatively good when compared to other inexperienced, poorly trained teachers, but the results are more problematic when they are compared to fully prepared and experienced teachers." Nonetheless, it does not mean TFA teachers cannot become great educators. The former Social Studies department chair at my high school worked in the corporate sector before joining Teach For America and becoming an alum of the program. She has now been an educator for over 10 years and was even named the 2022 North Region Teacher of the Year. Proof that some TFAs can learn, develop and hone their skills into becoming great teachers. Lastly, TFA teachers also become a major expense for local and state school budgets. Research by Heilig and Jez (2014) shows that "more than half of TFA teachers leave after two years, and more than 80 percent after three…Furthermore, the high turnover of TFA teachers results in significant expenses for recruiting and training replacements." Heilig and Jez (2014) further points out that these expenses "for teachers who constantly churn involves recurring financial costs. Districts also pay TFA a fee per corps member per year employed—resulting in a substantial on-going expenditure." In the example of the two social studies TFA teachers who were hired for the '16-'17 school year, one left after his second year and the other one did not return after his third year of teaching. So the question then begs to be asked: Are TFA teachers worth the continuous high turnover rate and expenses that are disadvantages and setbacks to our Black students and schools?

The second issue is that people with no educational background and experience are better decision-makers than those with years of frontline experience in the classroom. One obvious example is that politicians have a huge say in local, state, and national educational budgets and curriculums taught to students. The presumptuousness that these people make decisions or mandates that set the tone for how teachers should teach their students is ridiculous. A glaring example would be former Department of Education Secretary Betty DeVos, who was appointed by then President Donald Trump. Secretary DeVos has no experience, none whatsoever in education; but was appointed to run an agency that had a $71.5 billion budget for the fiscal 2019 year. Even according to Secretary DeVos own website (www.betseydevos.com), it talked about how she is a proven leader and advocate in education, business, and in politics. But in all honesty, she was appointed by President Trump because she is a Michigan billionaire who donated millions to the Republican party. DeVos is an advocate for school choice, primarily pushing for alternative or charter schools. Charter schools have become both an alternative to public schools, but also a major concern as well. A Washington Post article by Valerie Strauss (2017) states how DeVos "has made clear her K-12 priority is expanding charter schools— which are publicly funded but privately operated—and vouchers or voucher-like programs, which use public money to pay for private and religious schools in different ways. Her supporters say those measures offer parents more choices, but her critics say they drain resources from the public education system, the most important civic institution in the United States." Even during her Senate Education Committee confirmation hearing, DeVos could not discuss a key federal law protecting students with disabilities and could not discuss how student progress on standardized tests is measured. She was, however, later confirmed by the Senate, only because then Vice President Mike Pence became the first-ever vice president in American history to break a tie in a Cabinet nomination. Secretary DeVos was also known for making outlandish statements that are rooted in falsehood and ignorance too. Three weeks on her job as Department of Education Secretary, DeVos issued a statement on February 28, 2017, after meeting with Historical Black Colleges and Universities (HBCU) presidents stating:

"They started from the fact that there were too many students in America who did not have equal access to education. They saw that the system wasn't working, that there was an absence of opportunity, so they took it upon themselves to provide the solution. HBCUs are real pioneers when it comes to school choice. They are living proof that when more options are

provided to students, they are afforded greater access and greater quality. Their success has shown that more options help students flourish."

A statement that shows DeVos does not understand the true historical treatment of Blacks in the United States, especially in the South. Blacks were never given the same opportunities when it came to education in the South, both in funding, infrastructure, and resources as their white counterparts. HBCUs were founded simply because of racism and the refusal of white colleges and universities to admit Blacks into their institutions. So ironically, we had a person in charge of the Department of Education who was not a champion of public education, but envisions our K-12 school systems running as a business, and is ignorant to the significance and purpose of Historical Black Colleges and Universities.

The second example of this same issue of the notion of people with little to no educational experience making decisions would be the use of the *"Teach Like A Champion"* book series that so many school districts, principals, department chairs and academic coaches use to influence teaching in the classroom.

The author, Doug Lemov, has no educational experience as a teacher or in a classroom setting altogether. For it to be an educational book, it is mostly written through the educational experience and knowledge from observing one particular teacher, Darryl Williams, to compensate for his lack of firsthand familiarity and involvement in the classroom. Mr. Lemov is not an educator himself as stated on the Teach Like A Champion website. It clearly states that he "studies teachers". Interesting, because anyone can think that they are an expert by just studying or observing someone; but you truly become an expert in a field when you have hands-on experience for many years. Next, the Chief Academic Officer Erica Woolway says in her bio on the Teach Like A Champion website, she collaborates with the team to train teachers and school leaders…and wants everyone to know that she is a certified Chihuahua trainer and supposedly was the second choice for the character Elaine on the TV show *Seinfeld,* reportedly. Once again, a person with no direct classroom experience are the ones giving advice, writing educational books, and training those who are in the classroom. There comes some relief that their "team" has people who actually do have classroom and educational experience. Honestly, I have not read *Teach Like A Champion* and nor do I ever intend to. Opinions run high with educators who have many years of experience in the classroom that were given a copy of the book. They all questioned how this book garners such support even when the people promoting this book never stood in either an elementary, a middle or high school classroom. Ray Salazar, a 17-year teaching veteran when the 2011-2012 school year began, wrote about the obstruction that *Teach Like A Champion* is causing in school districts across the United States. He states that "Despite the author's view that these techniques put students on the path to college, this book perpetuates the culture of low expectations among low-income youth. The book glorifies teachers who do the minimum. In truth, these techniques are rudimentary classroom-management approaches—not championship teaching." (Salazar, 2011) Any good educator would tell you that having a successful school year and getting the most out of your students is by establishing effective classroom management. But the biggest predicament about having people in positions of authority or having books written by people with no educational experience is that they have a major voice in how our school systems operate. It is like a person who gives parental advice to parents but has never raised a child of their own. Or someone who gives marital advice to a married couple but is or has not been married themselves. In such a way, their advice should be taken with a grain of salt. But one glaring admittance about *Teach Like A Champion* is the pedagogical model that is very similar to the late 1800s to early 1900s in the United States. Layla Treuhaft-Ali (2017) writes "As I was reading Teach Like A Champion, I observed something that shocked me. The pedagogical model espoused by Lemov is disturbingly similar to one that was established almost a century ago for the express purpose of maintaining racial hierarchy." She explains how this was an initiative where rich white businessmen and philanthropists would fund and direct teacher education programs. Treuhaft-Ali further explains that "In the new capitalist social fabric, white teachers were educated to bring sophisticated writing and speaking skills and rigorous academic content to their students in order to train them to be business managers and civic leaders.

Meanwhile, Black teachers and students were taught that menial labor was their natural birthright. The result was a severe lack of academic training available to Black teachers—and, consequently, their students—which devastated Black secondary schools well into the 1950s and 1960s." Tanesha B. Forman (2020) expresses "My most deep-seated issue with the book is the lack of recognition of the profoundly flawed and inequitable systems that have created generational disparities along lines of difference, in particular, systems that have oppressed Black, Indigenous, and/or people of color (BIPOC). By ignoring systemic racism, the author bypasses history and presents techniques that are seeped in racist ideas about these communities." Furthermore, Forman also declares "This problem is exacerbated by bringing in techniques from Teach Like a Champion because of the need to "expedite" growth and learning. In too many cases, this looks like teachers entering communities as outsiders and imposing their will and power over students (because they are coached to) without a deep understanding of the community social contract." The overall principle objection to both the TFA model and the use of the

Teach Like A Champion book is that it puts teachers [individuals] who **(1)** are not fully certified or credible to teach or **(2)** don't have the understanding of being able to relate and teach our Black students without coming into the classroom with a "savior" mentality.

The third issue would be the hiring of inferior teachers in the classroom. The hiring of these teachers do more harm and damage than good for students that are sitting in the classroom in front of them every day. This has been a constant issue at my present high school in my ten years with the endless cycle of teachers who are inferior. The rationale for this varies, but perhaps the most defining factor would be the lack of classroom management. Whether you are a rookie or have some years under your belt, or a veteran, if you do not have good classroom management you will fail at this job or you will always feel burnt out at the end of each day. There are many definitions for the meaning of classroom management, but it simply means as the teacher you are in control of the classroom, you manage or discourage behavioral outbursts or problems by students, you foster a safe learning environment, you actively engage students, and most importantly, you know how to disseminate your lessons across the board to every student in a way that they all can learn. When I first began my educational journey as a substitute teacher in January 2006, I completed a two-day training course to learn all the inner workings of being a "temporary instructor". I did most of my substitute assignments at high schools, although I did substitute at both elementary and middle schools a few times. I did substitute teaching for a few years as I finished my bachelor's degree, worked on obtaining my Florida Educator's professional certificate, and probably most importantly just getting my life in order. Substituting gave me the opportunity to learn exactly what classroom management meant and what it looked like. One prime example of good classroom management or structure was noticing the way that students entered the classroom. Students would speak by saying "good morning" or "good afternoon", and then politely sit at their desk and minimize their movement and loud conversations, or even ask to use the restroom prior to class starting or after the first 15- or 20-minutes of class starting. But the important factor was that there were always detailed instructions/lesson plans of the assignment(s) that students were to complete in that teacher's absence. When in other classes, students either would stand or congregate in front of the classroom door, or come into the room all loud and boisterous, or even have their friends try to skip into the room because there was a substitute, and plus, I would be lucky if the teacher actually left an assignment that would be meaningful and not just "busy work". Busy work just simply kept them "busy" for about 10 minutes at best. It truly was a day-and-night experience in these classes where you could tell which class had a teacher who had a good management style and one who did not. Aside from poor classroom management, students are very quick to point out and voice their opinions when they have these inferior teachers. Students' biggest complaint is that these teachers give them assignments that are simply "busy work" from either the lesson or chapter review in the textbook, or an uninspiring and unengaging reading, math, or science packet. Students explain that these kinds of assignments do not challenge them to use any critical thinking skills. So what do students do…it's simple: complete the assignment for the easy grade and then retreat to their own little world of social media, games, music, take a nap, ask for a pass and walk the halls, or right before the end of class they will copy from their classmates. Nevertheless, students will always "spill the tea" about how these teachers do not do much in terms of teaching. Students clearly express how these teachers will just give the answers during class discussions or to the assignment mainly because they do not expect much or challenge their students to think, and therefore just give up. Students also quickly point out how the classwork is repetitive and useless in their educational development. But at the end of the day, students simply complete the work for the grade. Every year, I always ask my graduating seniors for their honest opinion on this very simple question: *Do you feel as though this school has truly prepared you for the real world?* Most of their answers are emphatically "NO!" mainly because most of their classes have been a waste of time in their own words or that these classes serve no purpose when they think about their future lives. Intensive math and intensive reading classes for standardized testing throughout their four years of school always ranks near the top of their responses. Students don't feel as if the school as a whole is preparing them for the real world, perhaps more prepared for real

world behaviors and attitudes, but not so much the necessary

skills. Whereas those students who have taken advanced

academic classes (Cambridge, AP or dual enrollment) feel better

prepared because of the collegiate rigors of those courses, and

they feel that those teachers care and invest more in them. But

inferior teachers cannot give up so quickly and easily in the

classroom. No matter how much training, preparation, and

education one has, it's not an easy road. Plus, I get it, these

teachers are usually first-year or early in their teaching career, or

new to the educational field altogether. So therefore, they are

usually given regular classes with rude, undisciplined, and just

ruthless students in either ninth or tenth grade. So how do you

help these teachers who have been labeled "inferior" because of

their lack of classroom management? To an extent, you must

pair them with tough, no-nonsense veteran teachers who can

walk them through the wildfire. Not necessarily hold their hand,

but gently guide them through the school year when it comes to

classroom management: discipline, grading, attendance,

engaging lesson plans and strategies, and parent contact. But at the same time, these inferior teachers must be willing to learn from veteran teachers. Lastly, students know and even name the teachers who are in the classroom only for the paycheck. They clearly know which teachers have the love and passion for this career versus those who just show up to get paid. If you're not happy and do not have the love and passion for this line of work…leave and find a new job instead of subjecting students to your unhappiness.

In closing, numerous issues and concerns were discussed about the troubling trends when it comes to educating Black students in today's society. But there must be genuine and modest discussions to understand these dangerous shifts in both education and the classroom. These are serious matters that must be addressed in the proper setting with respect, dignity, and decorum. The continuing of simple fixes using band aids or doing patchwork to cover up flawed ideologies will not work, nor will it yield long-term results and success for Black students in the classroom.

Chapter 2

This chapter will primarily focus on why *"great"* Black teachers leave our Black schools. In general, most teachers regardless of whether they are good or great are exiting the school system faster than large crowds that used to gather for Black Friday midnight sales before COVID. The reasoning behind this obviously starts with teachers' salaries. Teachers are still grossly underpaid compared to other professions; although we need teachers to teach those other professions. I will always stand by the argument that teachers deserve higher salaries not because I'm a teacher, but all the hats that have to be worn in the classroom. These hats include aside from preparing lessons and teaching, but for grading, motivating, counseling, being surrogate mothers or fathers, cheerleaders, career advisors, a shoulder to cry on, a confidant, or even give away our last snack, water/Gatorade or dollar to a student in need. Now mind you, as a high school teacher who has taught seven or all eight classes in a given year with an average of 25-30 students per class, I wear those hats multiple times a day and some at the same time. I would strongly challenge any person who dares to differ on this matter to please schedule a visit to my classroom and perform these duties any day of the year when you are available. Other reasons include being overworked (burnout) with class sizes and all the standardized testing, the lack of parental and administrative support and involvement, and then all the red tape that teachers have to deal with on an everyday basis. Furthermore, this chapter will highlight and express the thoughts and responses of six fellow educators to a questionnaire for transparency. Their years of experience range from 14 to 30 years in the educational field. Most have furthered their education with a Master's degree. They have also held several positions including department chair, curriculum support specialist in mathematics, school coordinator for Cambridge, test chair, academy/magnet lead teacher, and temporary assistant principal. One of them even taught for one year in the psych ward for juveniles. These are the following questions that they were asked along with their responses:

1. **What do you believe are some of the problems that educators face in the classroom today?**

Most of their responses to this question were similar in identifying problems in the classroom today. Disrespectful students who are unmotivated and not interested in learning, there is no accountability for student grades or actions, students also lacking both the critical thinking and prerequisite skills that are not taught on a widespread scale for important subjects, poor teacher salaries, and the continuous lack of support and respect from parents and administration. Valecia Beaufort adds that "People who are not in the classroom or in education at all, make decisions that impact the classroom/education. It is also financial spoils–too many programs being pushed for financial gain and not for academic progress." Tiffany Dallas stresses how there is "an overambitious and xenophobic governor [Ron DeSantis-FL] that whitewashes history to rectify white guilt." Michaelle Menard-Wagnac added that because students are not interested in learning and that they just copy and cheat their way through, and you also get students placed in advanced academic courses with the bare minimum. Lastly, these teachers also noted the struggles of dealing with students coming to school and classes smelling of weed, having personal hygiene issues, and not having good nutritional habits, whereas they are instead eating hot chips and sugary candies/snacks and drinks first thing in the morning and throughout the school day.

2. **What do you believe are the main reasons why good Black educators choose to leave the classroom or schools in Black communities?**

Their responses acknowledged once again both the lack of parental and administrative support and respect. They also questioned the lack of resources for students in laptops/tablets and books. However, a few teachers provided true, unfiltered hard lined answers to this question. Andrew Harris responded with "Administrators, parents and students treat Black educators with no respect for the job that they are doing…the frustration and disappointment in engagement from them breaks down good teachers over the years." Menard-Wagnac adds that "Teachers leave because the parents don't really advocate for their children's rights…(but) they will quickly run to the district offices to complain about foolishness like uniforms and completely ignore the facts about the shortage of books or teachers for core classes." Nevertheless, Dallas sums it up best: *"You get tired of giving your all to be met with consistent disrespect and lack of support. Then you wake up one morning and realize your career as an educator is more like an abusive marriage that you stay in for the kids. After the third mental breakdown, you start prioritizing your well-being, best interests and begin plotting your exit."*

3. What is your honest opinion about the usage of student data?

The use of student data is a hot-buttoned and controversial issue in schools depending on who you have this discussion with. I, however, am not a supporter of using student data because it is so highly subjective and manipulated to one's liking. An example being that one could have an 80% passing rate, but then one would become so completely fixated and caught up as to why the other 20% did not pass. But do you not see that 80% passed? Nevertheless, the responses were mixed from the teachers based on this question. Yet all agreed that data could be used to measure student learning gains and know their students' strengths and weaknesses in content to drive instruction. However, Beaufort states that student data "is absolutely a false narrative pusher and the numbers are manipulated to further disenfranchise our students and community." Dallas furthered the point by stating that "student data can be manipulated to illustrate any outcome needed. Data does not tell the whole story of student achievement. It is a snapshot in time." Sherwonda Saunders believes that student data "should only be used to increase their comprehension levels so they would be prepared to conquer society in reading, writing, arithmetic and social studies." Saunders also believes that student data should be limited to reading and math, if necessary, instead of testing students to increase the school's grade. "Standardized testing is trash!" was strongly echoed by Menard-Wagnac, who also believes we cannot base a child's future on a test. Both Josephine Galloway and Harris are strong believers of student data only if the data is collected and used correctly to improve student achievements and drive instruction. Galloway further states "the use of data lets you know areas that students are weak and also areas of students' strengths." Harris seconds this idea by saying "honestly, I love student data if the assessments given truly give an accurate reflection of the student's ability."

4. What can be done to educate our Black students in today's society?

In one accord, they all answered with very sharp and stinging critical responses as to how to solve this question. Both Beaufort and Menard-Wagnac believe that there should be a return to the core fundamental skills for students. Beaufort said to "go back to teaching foundational skills and make literacy the core of what we do, not passing a test. If students are not literate, then we will never yield the results we are aiming for." Menard-Wagnac furthers this sentiment by adding "we need to go back to a skill-based type of educational system. Students need to study and focus on areas of interest: college/university, vocational and technical trades, etc." Saunders' opinion is that students should be fed more History; give them more food for their brains by letting them know where they come from and where they should be heading. Galloway believes that students need to take a course(s) on how to be respectful, and that parents definitely need to do their part in helping to educate their children when they are young and insisting that they do their homework. Harris and Dallas both offered scathing remarks that summarizes why most Black educators leave the field and what could be done to reverse these unsettling trends. According to Harris:

"All Black schools need real structure and discipline that reflects zero tolerance for student conduct. Teachers are tired of students being disrespectful, using profanity at them and threatening them with no consequences for their actions. In addition, getting rid of Standard-Based Grading is very important because it gives our Black students a false sense of how much they really know. We push students through school to get funds from the government without properly educating them to have basic skills for society."

Dallas furthers the same attitude and sentiment:

"Public schools are failing our students. They promote mass indoctrination and values that are contrary for many within our communities. I believe we need to start our own schools, have more control over the curriculum we write, repair and foster

relationships within our centers of worship, community centers and parks...As long as we depend on a broken system, we will perpetuate the same broken system to continue. I can see mass defunding of Black schools in the future, and when that happens, what will be the next move then?"

In closing, there are no simple answers or easy fixes to these questions. To start, a few suggestions would be to level the playing field with accountability and zero tolerance of students' disrespectful behavior and their academics, a more streamlined approach to using student data, and finally the support, the cooperation and respect from both parents and school administration. There is too much red tape that teachers have to deal with when it comes to disciplinary actions for students and too much work, responsibilities, accountability and expectations in the classroom. Obviously, these changes will not occur overnight, but there has to be a starting point. Parents, students, teachers, and administration must all work together in one accord to have school-wide success for everyone in the school, and not just the chosen few.

Chapter 3

If there truly is an "X-factor" that has a significant impact on a school's culture and environment, teacher and staff morale, and the overall experience; then it would be the principal and his/her assistant principals. Administrators are a *Catch-22*. The majority of school administrators are a joy and great pleasure to work with because they have the right attitude and are supportive, and professional. And because of this, you love them to death and greatly appreciate them for their hard work. Whereas others simply become administrators who are either highly unqualified or use that position to flex their muscles becoming vindictive and mean-spirited to prove a point. Vengeful tactics such as these could be closely related to that of the late President Richard Nixon who used the highest office in the land to punish his political rivals. But many of these same administrators seem to have forgotten life in the classroom, or because they are still too young in their educational careers that they have not honestly earned their stripes yet. From having attended numerous professional development courses and conversing with other colleagues through the years, there is this notion that countless people get promotions within school districts with little to no experience in the classroom. With several of these people becoming curriculum support specialists, academic coaches, and administrators. These promotions are more of a "not *what* you know, but *who* you know" approach in districts.

Two main complaints of administration would be their lack of support in dealing with problems/concerns addressed by teachers and the miscommunication and organizational issues. The first complaint being that when teachers write referrals for students' disrespectful and misbehavior in class or academic misconduct, only to see that nothing has happened. Hell, most times that student is sent back to class minutes later or before the bell after being sent to the main office. Now some teachers do write referrals for ridiculous reasons, so I can understand why administrators would scratch their heads and send that student back to class. But when teachers write detailed and well-documented referrals and have made parent contact, then you need to do your job. Nevertheless, when these issues arise in the classroom, the proper support from administration is needed, or else teachers will ultimately look weak in the eyes of their students. Reason being because now students know they are in-charge and there will be no disciplinary actions. So now teachers lose in their mission to educate and foster a learning environment for students. Even as a veteran teacher, you still need the support of the administration on your side. However, there are times when they cannot be found, they are hiding in their offices with the doors closed, or just not completely interested in dealing with issues. But when you truly need them, whether you are calling their office extension or personal cell phone, it's as if they ghosted you! Therefore, you feel like you're stuck on a remote island with no life support, and then you see a boat in the near distance but it just keeps going, leaving you stranded. The support of administration is very important for teachers in the classroom and the school overall. A second example of the lack of support from administration would be through academic coaches. These academic coaches work very closely with administration and are mostly assigned to ELA (English-Language Arts), Reading, Science and Math departments. Their main responsibility is to assist/coach teachers and students in providing strategies and techniques to make scoring gains on standardized tests for their departments respectively. So although not lacking in a supportive role, these coaches do however have a strong voice and influence within their departments; plus they too have the same unrealistic expectations and marching orders from administration. So when testing assessments and/or progress monitoring assessment tests results do not come back as expected; you can imagine how interesting data chat conferences would be. Being a social studies teacher, I thank God that our department does not have an academic coach assigned. But academic coaches can be just as annoying, rude, and disrespectful as administrators. One such incident involved an academic coach who constantly harassed a first-year teacher by calling after-hours during the week and on weekends to talk about strategies and assignments. It's one thing to call occasionally with a suggestion or strategy for the upcoming week, but it is beyond professional when the issue is address between the union and principal.

The second complaint being the miscommunication and organizational issues. Dysfunction is more of the proper term.

Because over the past ten years had me guessing at times whether I was at a school that was professional, or on the playground during summer camp season. Now understandably everything is not the administration's fault or blame because some things are beyond their control or are confidential matters. First example includes the constant interruptions with endless announcements and being unorganized when handling teacher absences. Announcements made by the administration are the worst simply because they frequently happen and are drawn out in length. Administrators always want you to teach bell-to-bell, except these continual announcements interrupt classroom instruction itself. Now there are many reasons for announcements throughout the day over the P.A. system, but the worst culprit is when administration asks teachers to take a moment and check your emails for a list of students' names to send them either to the auditorium or media center. Yet only to interrupt just two minutes later and then proceed to read the entire list of student names. Why then not read the names during the first announcement instead of having a second interruption??? So now at this point, all learning has come to a stop. Second is when faculty meetings are held monthly. Our teaching contract stipulates 60 minutes, but at times administration starts these meetings late and therefore ends after the contractual time limit. In fairness, most of what is discussed at these meetings can be disseminated through emails quite honestly. Third example would be the lack of organization when it comes to teacher absences. In fairness, some teachers do call-in and take days off just to take them off. It's one thing if an emergency happens (child is sick, accident or car failure), that's life; or you truly need a mental health day. But even when just a few or a mass of teachers are out, administration goes into full panic mode like chickens with their heads cut off. Massive teacher callouts are the usual suspects being the days before holiday weekends or breaks, or homecoming weekends for either HBCU homecomings or football classics. So you would think that there would be a plan in place since these days are well-known in advance with no surprises. Unfortunately, that is not the case. Administration tries to be nice and asks teachers to assist them in opening their classrooms to hold these students. But when you or a few teachers are out, they then strike a different chord by stating that either the department chair, academic coach, or the teachers split the absent teacher's classes among the department. Not my problem, and more importantly, it's above my pay grade. But why is this a problem, two factors, finding substitutes and district policies. The first factor being that when your school doesn't have the best image or has disrespectful students, getting substitutes to come at all is a challenge. In ten years, my high school has only had a very small handful of consistent substitutes. So because of this, you're almost willing to accept/hire the weird types, the "don't give a damn" types, or the young ones just out of college who still think they are one of the high schoolers since they haven't been that far removed. Plus, some school districts have policies stating that substitutes can only work a certain number of days in the payroll period (i.e. 8 out of 10). Which now means the person at the school responsible for getting substitutes must be resourceful and strategic in scheduling substitutes for coverage. A factor that is both cost-cutting by districts and severely impacts instructional coverage in schools.

Finally, most of the assistant principals I have worked with the past ten years have been fairly decent. One assistant principal who later served as vice principal for a few years, was one whom I was not at all fawned of. Mainly because of their personality and just the way they came off at times. In my first year at the school, she was the assistant principal assigned to the social studies department. Ironically, she never attended a department meeting or provided support for our department too. But perhaps my biggest turn-off about her was one time at a faculty meeting, she read off names of a few people from a list asking to meet with her right afterwards. My name was one of them she calls, and I'm thinking in my head like why and what did I do? So when I go up and find out what she wants...she asked me, "Where did you go the previous week for professional development?" I answered her by stating that I attended a social studies PD at another school. So in my mind I'm thinking did I commit a crime by not attending the PD that was held at the school itself? But the whole time during this quick Q & A, she never once looked at me directly; making me feel almost like a "nobody", a lowly peasant. Again, it goes back to my opening statements about administrators, what point are you trying to

prove? After this encounter with her, I started to believe what

my other coworkers had said about her. However, if there is one

positive thing I can say about her is that she did help me in

strengthening my lesson plans in terms of explaining what the

outcome of the assignments would be that students were

completing. So instead of just providing the title of the

assignment, which is mostly written generically in the gradebook

by teachers but explains the purpose and reasoning behind it.

Since then, I have always written the purpose of the assignments

in my lesson plans, and I even started writing a narrative of each

assignment in the gradebook as well; so therefore, students and

parents would know and understand what each assignment was.

But perhaps the worst feeling is when you're surrounded by an

administration team that seems ill-prepared and mainly

incompetent. In these ten years, there have been one or two

administrators at times that fit this description; but only once has

that feeling seem to apply to the entire administration. First-time

administrators, a vice-principal who was obsessed with

data…data, data, data; everything was driven by data in her eyes no matter the circumstances. Overall, she was nice, but at times could be a snake and was unfortunately at times made out to be the "bad guy" when a certain principal did not want to be the culprit or get their hands dirty when it came to unfavorable situations. A second vice-principal was the true definition of inadequacy and incompetence to the highest degree possible in my opinion. I know we should not judge upon appearance, but she just gives off that Homer Simpson "Duh" resemblance. Therefore, giving the vibe of *"not what you know, but who you know"*. An example being when I sent an email to this administrator asking to have a student removed from AP U.S. Government simply because they were not cutting it. To my surprise, there was no reply or acknowledgement of this email or request. When passing by her the following day, no acknowledgement of the email whatsoever once again. So therefore, I had no choice but to ask the counselor to do the schedule change. Plus, what further infuriates me is when administrators who have no clear understanding of advanced academic courses (Cambridge, AP, dual enrollment) are not willing to accept feedback or suggestions from the coordinator(s) and teachers to further enhance these programs. I guess it is more of a move to not seem weak or get embarrassed by those who have the knowledge. Having taught Cambridge U.S. History AS Level for the past eight years with a very successful passing rate, I believe my opinion would have some weight when I spoke on the subject. Case in point, there was this *brilliant* idea to drop the AP World History option for 9th graders and put them in the Cambridge International History AS Level course. A move that was not well-thought out where you had forty students from 9th grade selected and set up for failure. The coordinator and I tried to explain to her that this was not a very good idea especially since the AS Level course is primarily for either 11th or 12th graders with a strong background in Cambridge. But it is just the complete lack of trust and unwillingness to listen and take into consideration that frustrates you as a teacher when dealing with an incompetent administrator. All teachers want their students to be successful, especially those of us who teach advanced academic courses, but at some point, a line has to be drawn where it is not feasible for that student's success. Therein lies the biggest issue when administrators with no background or willingness to learn about advanced academic courses seemingly do whatever they deem fit and are willing to place students in a "no win" situation especially when they do not have the academic or necessary skills to be successful.

At the beginning of this chapter, it was stated that not all administrators are bad; just as the same can be said about teachers too. However, administrators are held to an even higher standard and professionalism. They have the ability and authority to move the needle and get things done. Even though many of them fall short most of the time especially when it comes to supporting teachers and backing them when most needed. Additionally, administrators do not always have their teachers' back. They may say so, but most will support the student over the teacher at the first opportunity. Bureaucracy in public education continues to impede the growth and leadership within Black schools. The foremost factor being that administrators cannot or are limited in suspending or dismissing disruptive students from Black schools especially if it is their home school. It's a numbers game...to not be at the top of the district's list for having the most disciplinary actions taken.

Therefore, both administrators and teachers are at a disadvantage

with one hand tied behind their backs in dealing with student

discipline. However, in secrecy, Black schools have restrictions

placed on them in terms of the number of suspensions and

dismissals of students; whereas White schools do not have any

limitations when it comes to their disciplinary actions. The most

significant disappointment comes from knowing that White

schools can suspend or dismiss a student more, particularly

Black students, if he or she causes the first sign of trouble or if

the school is not their home school. Therefore, this is a list of a

few matters and reasons why administrators are that *Catch-22*.

Chapter 4

When the current school year ends in June 2024, it will mark ten years that I have taught at my present high school. I never thought I would have been here this long, nevertheless, I feel completely blessed, fulfilled, and humbled having worked there. I have had great, outstanding students. I have taught the siblings and cousins of former students, but I have also experienced the heartbreak with the loss of lives due to violence and suicide of these same students too. I have become that consistent and dedicated individual to these young men and ladies through the years. I also have a connection with many of them because of their family backgrounds from the islands of Jamaica, and Haiti, and the Bahamas predominantly, mainly because I am of Bahamian descent and my wife is of Jamaican descent. In these ten years, it has been fun and exciting times, although there have been questionable decisions made by administration, teachers, and students; but probably the saddest and most troubling was the loss of a coworker. This chapter will focus and spotlight *"Life in the Classroom"* with the trials, the tribulations, and heartaches of working as a Black male teacher.

The Asylum Runs the Yard (2014-2019)

In my ten years, I have worked with four principals who all seemingly shared and promoted a sense of family first, as well as the philosophy that if you do your job, nobody will bother you. Although the fourth principal seems not to share these same beliefs to a degree primarily because of being a micromanager. Every principal has different managerial styles and makes decisions that may not always be favorable by the faculty and/or students. But of course, it comes with the territory. I am very grateful to the first principal, Mr. Williamsport, who hired me and gave me this tremendous opportunity to work at this high school. I was very tempted to stay working at a K-8 Center where I was teaching 8th grade Advanced American History, however, the principal there had different ideas. Despite this, I loved working at that school as a 3100 (temporary instructor), great coworkers and students, and a wonderful atmosphere. But my move to the high school was the perfect calling for me mainly because it saved on gas, mileage, and tolls to get where I previously worked; now it was only a 10-

minute drive to work. Working for this principal was truly a learning experience for me. I felt as though I was truly giving back to my community by working there, even though I did not grow up in the surrounding neighborhood, but in the Allapattah neighborhood. I never went in thinking I was going to be a savior, but the goal was to try and educate as many Black students who sat in front of me and teach them at a high standard and never lower my expectations that I knew they could achieve and accomplish if they were pushed. My first year (2014-2015) had me teaching U.S. History to 11th graders with an End-of-Course (EOC) exam that May. On the first day of school, the air conditioner was not working in my classroom, and since I was hired right before the new school year started, I had not been inside this classroom the week prior. So there is no definite answer as to how long the air conditioner had not been working in this classroom. Which of course would be completely unacceptable during the dog days of summer in July and August anywhere. Because of this A/C failure of not working for quite some time and the heat and humidity, mold began to grow on one wall inside the classroom. So because of that, I had to move to another classroom for five months until the unit was fixed. Mainly there was no rush really because this was the second to last year of a fifty-year-old school building, and considering we were moving into a brand-new school in two years. Aside from this circumstance, I had my first rodeo in understanding subject area accountability courses, and the importance of those courses and its impact on a school's grade. Suffice to say, the students I had did well, but not at the percentage I guess was needed to help improve upon the school grade. Many of my students who did not pass were within 10 points of the passing score, simply meaning if they answered one or two questions correctly, they would have passed. I viewed it somewhat as a success especially for my first year, but as I said, in terms of passing rate, then no. It then became that eye-opening experience for me in grasping the seriousness of it. I was in the big leagues. That following school year (2015-2016), I was demoted to 9th grade World History; although the message relayed to me was they wanted a strong, disciplinary teacher for the incoming freshmen class that year, it was more because of my students' performance on the EOC the year before in my opinion. That's the way I interpreted it. I was disappointed, but I did not make any noise or complained. I simply came to work that second year and continued to work hard knowing that I would one day return to teaching upperclassmen once again. In staying humble, the next year (2016-2017), I was given an advanced class to teach called Cambridge U.S. History AS Level. I had never heard of Cambridge at this point, although I was very familiar with Advanced Placement, dual enrollment, and Honors classes. It was definitely a steep learning curve for me in understanding the Cambridge curriculum. I was given a mentor through the Advanced Academics department where I was assigned to a teacher who had been teaching Cambridge for some years and had a successful passing rate with their students. By the end of the year and having attended a Cambridge History AS Introductory training, I then felt comfortable and confident in my instructional delivery and preparing my students for their exam. That first year of me teaching Cambridge saw only two students pass, which was a remarkable improvement given that none passed the previous years; but the two who were successful both passed with a grade of "A". Now currently in my eighth year of teaching Cambridge, I am a seasoned veteran at teaching this course with mastery of the content, and understanding the writing techniques that are needed. Lastly, I have been successfully averaging a 70-80% passing rate for my students.

Towards the end of the 1st quarter of that same 2016-2017 school year, I was asked by Mr. Williamsport to do him a huge favor and return to teaching upperclassmen. More importantly, U.S. History for 11th graders, but the Cambridge version of that course. The teacher who was teaching these Cambridge courses was a first-year teacher who also was a TFA. Pretty much two strikes against these students. At that moment I had one Cambridge course for the true Cambridge students at the school who had taken other Cambridge courses in 10th grade and continuing in 11th and 12th grades to receive their AICE diploma and the Florida Bright Futures Scholarship, in addition to their high school diploma. The rest of my classes were World History for 9th graders. Although there was a little regret having those 9th grade students switched to that teacher whose classes I was now taking over, I had no remorse with the opportunity to return to teaching upperclassmen. Now this change brought the spotlight and some pressure on me from administration because the district had its eye on the school because of the large number of students registered to take Cambridge courses.

Administration had decided to register both 11th and 12th graders who were low level readers according to assessment test scores into this course. In my first three years of teaching the Cambridge version of U.S. History to these 11th graders and then 12th graders, I realized most of these students didn't have the basic skills that made my job much more difficult than it should have been. I have no problem teaching or going the extra mile to help students learn the Cambridge way, but when I spend more time teaching students how to do basic writing and critical thinking, it is very time-consuming. More importantly during those first three years (2017-2019) of me teaching Cambridge, my school wanted much of the "general population" in Cambridge classes, meaning—a dumping ground. In the advanced academic realm, there is Cambridge, Advanced Placement, dual enrollment, and Honors. Therefore, you would not think there would be 30 kids sitting in seven of my eight Cambridge classes especially if they were Levels 1 and 2 on these assessment reading and writing exams. You would have your Levels 4 and 5 in a course that is more collegiate rigor and offers students the opportunity to earn college credit for History. Not the case at my high school. I spent those three years teaching an advanced academic course to Level 1 and 2 students, and some Level 3 students who possibly could not understand what was required for Cambridge. For two years I taught all eight periods…teaching four 90-minute class blocks every day. Yes, the additional supplements for teaching those two extra classes were nice when payday came around, but at the end of each school year I was exhausted from giving my all. I did completely agree with Mr. Williamsport and his philosophy, "Why can't our students have the same advanced, rigorous collegiate-level courses like at the white schools?" An argument that no one from the district was willing to challenge and appear racist. However, where I differed was on the fact that those same highly advanced collegiate-level courses are NOT for everyone. So with that idea, low level students were routed through Cambridge instead of taking the U.S. History EOC class. Now in his defense, our school wasn't the only one doing this approach, there were other schools doing this egregious strategy too. The reason I know this is because when I have attended Cambridge workshops held by the district, a few teachers have stated how the wrong set of students at their schools were assigned Cambridge courses too. However, I do truly believe my school took it to the extreme. So when you have almost 200-300 students taking Cambridge History exams at $90 per student that the school district pays for in advance; simple math…$18,000 to $27,000 per year spent for three years. Plus, not to mention the school added Cambridge Biology exams too, where another 200 students were assigned. So when the school's testing data for the U.S. History EOC is above 90% passing rate for about 125+ students who took the exam, but the school's average reading scores are in the 30-40 percentile for all students in 11th or 12th grade. It does not take a genius to see the pattern and question the legality or better yet the morality of what was being done. Ultimately, I do feel that a disservice was given to most of those students who were registered in Cambridge History classes just simply because they did not have the academic ability, nor the skills to comprehend and master the curriculum that was required of them. Nevertheless, there were some Level 3 students who did benefit from Cambridge, and more importantly, were able to successfully pass the exam. At the end of the day, I understood what he was doing, but it doesn't mean it was right though.

Now in fairness, Mr. Williamsport was no dummy. He had that intellectual and street-hustler mentality that made him absolutely loved by students and faculty. He was a family-first principal, he took very good care of his teachers as long as you were on his good side, he had successfully trained many assistant principals who became principals themselves and was well-liked within the district. He was so well-liked and highly thought of that he was being groomed to perhaps become a regional superintendent or possibly higher in the district ranks. But then unfortunately some bad decisions including a relationship (then marriage) with a teacher, and then the events of May 2019 had probably done him in. Regardless, there was a lot of good that happened under him, school pride and spirit were at its greatest during his years while in charge. As a teacher, you loved working for him, and you loved coming into work every day.

There were pep rallies just about every time you turned around, he was all in favor of having faculty Christmas and end of the school year celebrations, student functions/activities and field trips, he provided good leadership and was very easy to approach and go talk to, and allowed students to have *"Fun Fridays"*, where students paid $2 to dress out of uniforms and attend a dance in the cafeteria during the last block one Friday each month throughout the year. The money collected from those Fun Fridays would help pay down the costs for senior activities and end-of-the-year grade level field trips to either Walt Disney World, Universal Orlando Resort or Busch Gardens. Either way there were flaws on the surface. There were countless times when there seemed to be no discipline within the school, as if the students ran the yard. Uniform and lockout policies were an absolute joke in terms of its implementation. Students genuinely never had a fear of repercussions because there really were none. You cannot do uniform checks and lockouts (hall sweeps) once or twice one week and then wait another 2-3 months later. There were incidents where guns were found on campus. One such incident had occurred three months into the opening of our brand-new $42 million dollar school in early November 2016, where a gun was found in a car in the student's parking lot. What started as a Code Yellow about 7:45 A.M., quickly turned into a Code Red lockdown for over the next four hours. I remembered students simply bored out of their minds, having to go to the restrooms, and classroom searches (mine being one of them) by the police, and police dogs who were sounding off with baritone barks in the hallway. My classroom was searched simply because the gun was found in the vehicle of a student presently sitting in my room. The student was arrested, although the gun was not his; but the student who did own the gun was arrested too. Nevertheless, inconsistency will lead to the asylum knowing that they have the control and make the decisions. Administration would sometimes dismiss written referrals by teachers and even willing to do grade changes for seniors to ensure their graduation. As unmanageable and disorderly as things might have appeared, as long as you did your job and were not an issue, you were left alone.

Continuing my years under Williamsport, the Class of 2019 (and 2020) will always have a soft spot in my heart mainly because they were that 9th grade class of students I taught in my second year at the school. For whatever reason, this class was responsible for events that occurred during their freshman year that consistently put the school on the news for all the wrong reasons. Some of these occurrences included students killing one another, an alleged night school rape, fights, and even where one student jumped off the catwalk at the old school. These were great students coming from all walks of life with great personalities and promising futures, but there were a few who chose different paths. Probably the headshaking moments that year were the number of cases where students were arrested and charged with murder. The first case being a young man accused of shooting and murdering a rabbi who was visiting family from New York. It took some time before an arrest was made, but as detectives were building their case, I remembered the principal coming to my classroom one morning and asking for this young man's student folder. It was mainly to show that he was not coming to class and hence his student folder would reflect that, and it would support the number of absences in the gradebook for my class. If there is truly one piece of advice for any educator, especially if you're new to the classroom…attendance is very important!!! Your gradebook is a legal document that can **_and_** will be used in a court of law. So if a student is absent from your class and commits a crime, but you mark them present, you will have to explain that to administration and the police. Documentation is very important, even documenting the time a student arrives to class late whether they have an official pass or not. But in the case of this young man, charges were later dropped by the state attorney's office simply because of insufficient evidence. Ironically enough, after he was released, he returned to the school two years later and you guessed it…he was enrolled in my U.S. History class. Suffice to say, he was only enrolled for a few weeks and then withdrew from the school. The second case involved another student who shot and killed a cousin at the family house on a Saturday night. He was arrested shortly afterwards but was released and came to school that Monday morning. But what was so weird about that following Monday morning was as I was walking down the hallway towards the main office to sign in, and just like in the movies, everything and everyone simply just blurred out, and I only noticed him walking for some reason. It wasn't until later that morning that I found out that he was arrested again by police. How I found out was because a young lady who normally enters my classroom very energetic and bubbly, came in very quiet and sad because he was arrested again. The third case was one that really shocked me just simply because of the brutality of what happened. This case involved a young man who was a C-average student, but well-behaved at least in my class. Although he did not always complete his assignments, he would sit next to my desk and just want to talk. No big deal, it was something he had done most of the school year anyway. But I was utterly surprised to hear on the news and see his mugshot as one of three people arrested for shooting another student twenty times. Twenty times??? Just completely downright numbed over all these tragic shootings by students of mine.

Another incident that made the news and again shined a negative light on the school once more involved a 9th grader claiming that she was raped by another 9th grader during night school. Both parties involved were students of mine, but in different periods. Now what is ironic about this whole situation is that 9th graders cannot register for night school. Why? Because they are just starting their high school journey, so therefore, they are not missing any credits or in need to make up credits. So apparently this young lady was telling her mom that she needed night school, but obviously she had other plans after school. I remembered one morning I was teaching, and both the young lady and her mom knocked on my door. What made this moment so awkward was that the young man whom she accused of raping her was in the classroom, and you could see him sitting in view while the door was opened. It was one of those "Twilight Zone" moments where you are not exactly sure what will go down. Either way, the young man was arrested, but ultimately the charges were dropped.

Fights are nothing new in high school. Disagreements or sometimes just sheer pettiness gets emotions going and a fight breaks out. It is also no secret that social media and bullying have led to an uptick in school fights too. According to the teacher's contract, teachers are not required to break up fights. I learned the hard way unfortunately when breaking up a fight between two of my students in the hallway right outside my classroom one time. My class had just returned from the media center where they picked their classes for 10th grade and were sitting patiently through the last 10 minutes of class before the bell rang. Apparently this one student became impatient and started mouthing off and I told him to "just sit down and relax yourself". He then proceeds to get up and walk out the classroom, and one student who simply just said, "you're not going to talk to my teacher like that" and went right out the door after him and a fight started. So I went out there to stop this fight with the assistance of two neighboring teachers. In the process of pulling them apart, one of the teachers grabs one of them and, like the Incredible Hulk, just swung the entire line of us from one side of the hallway to the other. So after everything calms down and the bell rings, and I'm writing the referral for the fight, the adrenaline wears off and then my entire left side of my body is throbbing in pain and hurting. I was in so much pain that I could not sleep in my own bed that I slept slouch over the couch that night. Even after trying to take Tylenol and/or Aleve to ease the pain, I had no choice but to report this pain I was experiencing from breaking up the fight and file workman's comp. But what was so crazy about this whole ordeal was that it all went down the last week of school before spring break. So after seeing the district's workman comp's doctor and prescribed painkillers, I had to use the aid of a walking cane to get around school those last few days. I even recalled one day coming back from getting lunch because I had the last block off, it took me over 15 minutes to walk from the teacher's parking lot to my classroom in the second building. So during this entire 15-minute walk, the bell ending lunch had rang and I just stood against the wall telling students to simply go around me. In addition, Mr. Williamsport was mopping the floor because of a spill and cracked a joke on me telling me to "take your goddamn time and don't slip and fall". Then on the last day before spring break starts, I'm hobbling down the hallway towards the main office and I see two boys who at first glance look like they were play-fighting until one of them got slammed and then it was on, and I'm like "all shit, really?!" So I'm slowly making my way down the hallway and yelling at them to stop. Luckily, they did stop, and I had one student walk one of them to the office while the other walked with me. So after having a few more doctor appointments, having an MRI performed, and physical therapy for about two months. I was thankful that it was just a real severe case of back spasms and a pinch nerve, no damage and everything got better as time went on. After that experience, I swore off completely that I would never, NEVER break up another fight ever again. I was so serious about it that it became a part of my introductory PowerPoint to every class at the beginning of each school year afterwards. I simply state "that if you fight in my class, you better know how to fight because I'm not stopping it unless one of you gets knocked out…it's not in my contract to stop fights". A mantra I hold true to this day.

Finally, the most bizarre moment of that school year happened shortly after the 2nd quarter began when a young man for whatever reason decided to jump off the catwalk between the first and second buildings on the west side of the school. I remembered that day because I stayed after school ended to grade papers, and then all of a sudden, I heard sirens and a helicopter hovering above the school. I start thinking to myself that I'll just stay a little longer. At this moment, I don't know what has happened yet, but then my phone rings, it's my wife calling and asking me if I know what just happened at the school. I told her no, so then she told me that a student had jumped from the catwalk, and I'm like "WTF???" So I started checking the local news stations' websites to find out what happened, and sure enough, a student had indeed jumped. The young man did survive this jump, however. About two months later he returned to school and was being wheeled to my classroom by a teacher in his wheelchair. As class got underway, it did feel weird and so uncanny to see him in the classroom sitting in his wheelchair considering what had happened to him earlier, and plus all the running jokes that were made about him too. But the cherry on top was that I had to serve him a student failure notice because he had an "F" in the class with two weeks remaining in the 2nd grading period. So after class ended, he asked why he was getting a failure notice and began to explain his circumstances. I simply told him that I understand your circumstances and explained to him that he was excused from those assignments; however, he had an "F" before this incident had happened. So I unfortunately had to serve him that failure notice.

No matter how many years you work in the classroom, you are bound to have some wild, crazy and unforgettable moments that you will always remember. Perhaps the most memorable and surreal event to ever happen occurred on May 8, 2019, during the spring testing season. So Mr. Williamsport had this somewhat ingenious idea at the beginning of the school year to have all testing done in the gymnasium in an effort to minimize school shutdowns and movement of teachers and students in terms of moving to different classrooms. His vision behind the thought made sense, however, the execution backfired on that day. So this would be the final year of almost 300 students, both 11th and mostly 12th graders, taking the Cambridge version of U.S. History in order to avoid having them take the EOC version which impacts the school's grade. The Cambridge History exam is a two-part written exam. Paper One was a 60-minute exam and Paper Two was a 90-minute exam under the old 9389 syllabus that ended in 2021. So on that uneventful day, the morning FSA testing session was ending and those students were exiting the gym, and the Cambridge students were entering the gym to prepare for their 12:30 P.M. exam. As the students were being seated throughout the gym, the collection of book bags and cell phones from each pod of students was also underway. I was collecting book bags from the pod of students in the middle of the gym when I noticed a commotion and a little circle starting to form. Anyone who teaches or works with kids knows that when you see a circle being formed, you know something is about to go down. Lo and behold, I noticed two students of mine from different classes started talking smack and putting up their hands [fists] and started fighting. *Backstory to this fight: one young lady was fighting for her cousin because she was continuously being bullied by the other young lady and her friends; even though all of this was reported to administration.* So I quickly started putting the book bags on the designated table and hurried over to break up this fight. Even though I swore that I would never break up another school fight considering what happened to me as I stated earlier in this section. Nevertheless, I ran over there to help break up this fight along with another teacher. Just as I was about to jump in, I noticed to the right of me a young lady, the cousin being bullied, standing on a chair and spraying this orange-colored mist overhead that is raining down inside the circle of the fight. When I abruptly stopped in my tracks, I slipped on the gym floor because of this mist and luckily, I did not get tramped over by students witnessing the fight who started running themselves. Then the young lady proceeds to come into the circle and continue spraying this orange mist towards the two girls fighting and the teacher who had grabbed one of them. I was in a state of shock and dazed as to what I was witnessing, it was as if time had frozen like once again in the movies. Only following this aftermath had I learned that the orange mist was bear repellent. Bear repellent…I ain't no damn animal from the forest!!! Although the local news stations reported it as pepper spray, that simply was not the case. I never witnessed the clearing of the school's gymnasium so fast ever. So many students and teachers were affected by this bear repellent incident that the main office of the school was turned into a triage, and there were at least eight fire rescue ambulances outside the main entrance to the school. Never in my life had I ever been pepper sprayed before, let along with bear repellent. But just the idea of being sprayed with a chemical deterrent that wards off bears in the wilderness was used on school grounds still to this day is beyond mind-blowing. The eye burning from the repellent was at its worst when I finally got home and took out my contact lenses. It was only then when I truly experienced these effects because my contact lenses had shielded my eyes. So pretty much the Paper Two exam was canceled and postponed until the following week with very strict procedures in place for students entering the gym. The repercussions from this event were that all three young ladies were suspended from school, and criminal charges were filed against the young lady with the bear repellent. I was even contacted by the state attorney office to ask if I was willing to testify when this case would come to court. However, five years has passed since this event, no such luck or news about the outcome of this incident to my knowledge. A memorable occurrence that will truly forever be in my mind.

Now if that previous occurrence was the cherry on top, the final incident of my first principal's era was truly a heartbreaking experience that I know in my heart still hurts the faculty and staff who used to work here or have retired, or those of us who continued to work here since. Ironically enough this devastating occurrence happened only the next week after the gymnasium incident. It involved the tragic murder of the beloved test chair by the just recently transferred assistant principal. Out of respect for all parties involved, discretion will be used in retelling this event. As everyone is still processing the bear repellent event from the previous week, testing had resumed at the beginning of next week. When the test chair did not report to work for a second day, which was the next scheduled testing day; most of the administration and faculty thought at first, she really, really needed a few mental days for herself. However, her absences became a serious concern when she did not answer phone calls or emails from the school and co-workers. There was such a concern for her that a missing person's report was filed with the police, and her missing was aired on local news stations and printed in the newspapers. She was an overall genuine and lovable person. If she asked you for a favor or to proctor an exam, you could not say no to her.

Plenty of times throughout the year I am used as a proctor. She once told me the main reason that I use you to proctor is simply because I can trust you and not have any issues. Hell, one time during testing she even put me in charge of the "master laptop" where I oversaw the entire testing group of students for the last 20 minutes of a test session. A statement of faith and trust. But her disappearance, and ultimately murder still leaves a hole in everyone's heart who knew her. Now because of social media, multiple rumors and stories were running rampant all around the school. I had heard just about all of them, some could make sense, and a few were farfetched. Two moments that stood out between her missing, and subsequently being found murdered and the arrest of the former assistant principal were a school field trip and the 2019 graduation. The first moment was when the school club I sponsored returned from Universal Orlando Resort late Friday night on May 24th. What was strange about our return to the school around 11:15 P.M., me and three other teachers who served as chaperones noticed someone going in and out of the main front doors of the school. It was hard for us to get a good look at who the person was or what they were carrying and loading up because the chartered bus dropped us at the end of the main building where the entrance gates were located, and plus we're making sure all 40 students who went on this field trip were picked up by their parents. Yet, you must ask yourself who is moving things/items this late on a Friday night? The second moment was at the graduation for Class of 2019. Graduation of course is one of the happiest moments and memories for seniors and their families. By this time, I had attended a few graduations from previous years to know when something seems off. First, when Williamsport introduced his administration, feeder-pattern schools' principals, and other distinguished guests; he introduced this one gentleman who was the school board attorney. The hell???? In previous graduations I attended, I had never in my life ever seen or heard of this person before. Why would the school board attorney be present at a high school graduation? Perhaps to make sure nothing is said relating to the test chair's death and criminal investigation. I only say this because secondly, he did make a public statement asking for a moment of silence in her honor. However, it just felt as if he wasn't supposed to make any mentions of her, even though this brief gesture and moment were genuine. Ultimately, the most important and biggest question that has yet to be answered is "Why?" At the time of publishing this book (June 2024), it will be five years from May 2019. Perhaps the most mind-boggling thing is that the trial has not even begun yet. Yes, COVID-19 created a backlog within the judicial system. However, when looking up the court case in county public records, there has been an astonishing 1,192 dockets between the first court appearance and hopefully a trial date set for June 17, 2024. It is amazing to think that it will be five years since her murder that a trial will finally take place. It is also cynical to believe that many people (administration and former teachers) have just removed and detached themselves from this tragedy thinking that transfers or relocations will shield them from justice. As interpreted from the Bible in Luke 12: 2-3, *"what is done in the dark shall come to light."*

A New Beginning (2019-2021)

It comes to no surprise that a change in leadership was made for the upcoming school year considering what happened to end the previous year. The second principal had served as the middle school principal across the street for most of the student body currently enrolled at the high school, including the incoming freshmen. This new beginning was much needed and welcomed. Although starting anew, things were very different. Mr. Lexington understood that our school family was still continuing to deal with the shocking murder just three months ago that was still so raw in our hearts and minds. There were quite a few teachers and staff who either left on their own accord or were given an involuntary transfer to another school. The new school year had an aspiration of new hope and a fresh start. Mr. Lexington continued in the same family-first approach as the first principal did, but the school's culture and environment had a different vibe. I believed he was the right person for the right moment, he understood what had taken place the last few years, and he was trying to right the ship. One thing that stood out was that he stated there would be no more overloading the Cambridge program with students who did not deserve to be there. He said regardless of what was done the last few years, no matter how unethical it might have been and those who were subjected to this practice [mainly myself], it was no longer going to continue. This became a huge weight lifted off my shoulders because I would no longer be subjected to teaching 6 to 7 Cambridge U.S. History classes for the masses. So my new teaching assignment was U.S. Government Honors and Economics w/ Financial Literacy Honors, in addition to the one Cambridge class for students who were in the school's Cambridge program. As the school year progressed, all the new changes that were implemented became a part of the daily routine. Perhaps the biggest and most serious event to occur that school year was the shutdown of schools and the world because of COVID-19. [Chapter 6] But one very special moment that happened prior to the shutdown occurred at a faculty meeting in late February 2020. A special education teacher was retiring after over 30 years of service and was honored at this meeting. Mr. Lexington said something so poignant that it became another mantra that I live by today as an educator. He said, "*teachers give so much of their time and themselves to their students, but never have that same kind of energy for their own families (children) when they get home.*" When I tell you that that quote had such a powerful and emotional impact on me…my entire thought-process literally changed after hearing that. At that moment, I would not overburden or overwork myself at work again. I would still give students my very best when in the classroom, but never again would I allow myself to take on more opportunities than necessary at work. Although I have three children now, I seriously thought about how I was shortchanging my own two children at the time. How on so many occasions I would go home too tired to really spend time with them. I was constantly asking God for that extra gear or burst of energy to just even take them to the park and let them run around and explore nature.

After two years at the helm and providing leadership through COVID, Mr. Lexington received a promotion and took a new position with the region for the district. While two years would seem too short, he was a good principal. He was able to start changing the culture that had been rampant the prior five years. Although there was one activity that did occur under him where he had his assistant principals at times stakeout the teacher parking lot in the back of the school to see if teachers were leaving before their contractual time. A little childish and petty in my eyes, but this kind of occurrence was not a new thing as I had heard from other teachers that their principals had resorted to these kinds of tactics as well. Ironically enough, the first principal, Mr. Williamsport, had talked about this same kind of activity at one of his final faculty meetings saying how he could have been the type of principal who stakes out in the parking lot; something he spoke to that his predecessor did when he was an assistant principal before his promotion at the same school. A former social studies teacher who retired at the end of the 2020-2021 school year was caught once leaving out of the parking lot at about 2:25 P.M. The next day he was called into the vice principal's office to talk about "stealing time from the district" because he left before 2:30 P.M. Although he was in the wrong since our teacher's contract says our work hours start 10-minutes before and end 10-minutes after the official school time of 7:20-2:20. To which he said, "I'm not stealing time, I'm at work in my classroom by 6:45, if anything, you should be paying me time that I arrive early". The satire in all of this is that on teacher workdays, no administrator arrives at the school before

8:00 A.M. I speak to the truth because my previous classroom window was above the administrators' parking spaces in the front of the school until I had to move three doors down. So I was always able to tell which administrator was in the building. Nonetheless, there was still room for improvement, and I truly believe that if Mr. Lexington would have stayed a third year, there would have been a thorough house cleaning to occur at the school. So for the third time in four years, there would be a new principal to lead the school. The person chosen to lead next would not be a stranger to many of us who have been at the school for at least the past six years.

The Soured Homecoming (2021-2022)

When you have worked at a school long enough, you will go through a cycle of principals and assistant principals. You are really lucky when a well-liked and loved former assistant principal returns as the new principal. That was the case of the third principal who was both an assistant principal and vice principal under the first principal. Upon his departure at the end of the 2015-2016 school year, Mr. Austin became principal himself, and an opportunity would have it that he would return four years later and become the principal where he previously worked. As I stated in the previous section, *A New Beginning*, it was a breath of fresh air and a much-needed change working for Mr. Lexington those two years. But the hire and return of the third principal, Mr. Austin, it felt like a return to old times comparable to Mr. Williamsport, the first principal, but without all the unnecessary drama. For many of us who had been at the school long enough, his return was a celebration like homecoming at a Historical Black College and University (HBCU). I remember greeting Mr. Austin with a handshake and open arms on the first day back to work for teachers. I remember talking to him about my family and showing him pictures and informing him during late October/early November that I was going to be taking a two-month paternity leave for the birth of my third child. He was a man of faith and family. Just as the two previous principals, family was first and foremost and very important. Unfortunately, this celebrated homecoming ended sourly after only one year at the helm. Now I cannot completely say with 100% accuracy as to why his stint was only for one year, but these are my suggestions. Although there were flaws and the "ball" was ultimately dropped by those in trusted positions; however, the school grade was still a "B" under his leadership. Probably one of the toughest jobs of being a principal are the constant meetings (budget, data chats, attendance, etc.) that they are required to attend. It's unfortunate because principals are not really in the building as much as you would think. I remembered on a teacher's workday in September, he was walking around and going classroom-to-classroom greeting everyone. When he came to my room, we talked for about 5 minutes on how things were going. He stated, "that when you're the principal, you really don't get the time to walk around and greet everybody as much as you like because you're always having meetings to attend." Obviously, that comes with the territory and the position. He was a good principal and really just a great, all-around good person. Perhaps the problem was that he was such a good guy, that he had too much trust and faith in those whom he left in charge. Throughout that school year in my true honest opinion, I undoubtedly believed that most of his administrative team failed him spectacularly in their job performances that year. If you were to give them a grade, it would unequivocally be "F3F". Unquestionably these administrators just did not give a damn at times when there were issues or problems. However, in fairness, I do believe one assistant principal did do his best to help resolve issues and any other concerns. This assistant principal would be working so hard that you would literally see the sweat falling from his face. Student discipline never seemed consistent as teachers were pretty much left on an island to handle these issues on their own. One matter was the never-ending and continuous fights among students throughout the year. Most school fights start ramping up as the year comes to an end, unfortunately, that was not the case. It seemed almost every day either in a classroom or hallway, at lunch or after school there was a fight going down. One fight that occurred after school one day had led to a student being shot one block away from the school. This young man had to be airlifted to the local trauma hospital and luckily, he did survive the shooting. But the true disappointment about this shooting was that it occurred three days before Christmas [winter] break. Another matter that resurfaced once again was an inappropriate relationship between an administrator and a teacher. There really is no secrecy when you have the prying eyes and gossiping of students and other teachers, even though you try your best to keep the relationship private. But nevertheless, it was not just all administrators, there were some teachers and other staff doing what they wanted to do when he was not there. One example being of teachers unlocking the parking lot gates and leaving them open and not locking them back for safety reasons. Therefore endangering everyone from faculty, staff and students because now anyone can walk or drive onto campus. Even during a faculty meeting, the principal spoke about how his bosses would inform him that they were on campus and no one, security or staff, stopped to question who they were. Ever since the deadly school shooting at Marjory Stoneman Douglas High School in Parkland (FL) on February 14, 2018, school security has once again become a serious priority in schools throughout the country. Although I still feel that at times that school districts are still playing games a bit and not really taking things seriously. Many teachers will probably tell you that guns undoubtedly are found on campus but are not

made aware of these situations until much later, if at all.
Nonetheless, with all these incidents and matters occurring, Mr.
Austin's tenure as principal ended after only one year. As the
saying goes, "the good suffers with the bad", unfortunately that
is what happened to a very good man.

The New *"Gilded Age"* of Leadership (2022-2024)

Another new school year brings a new principal and new
leadership. If you have worked in administrative or district-level
positions for many years, you will earn a reputation about
yourself whether good or bad. So the new principal, Mrs.
Sacramento, had a reputation of being a micromanager.
Micromanaging is understandable for certain fields of work, but
in a school setting, especially in a high school will cause
headaches and teacher fatigue. My first encounter of this
micromanaging was during our opening of schools meeting
where it's just this endless 3-4 hours of nonstop rambling talk by
administration going over the first day and first week of school
procedures. If you're a veteran teacher who has done multiple
openings of schools in your career, then all of this is just really

wasted time that could be used to finish setting up your classroom. So during this meeting, the fourth and new principal starts reading the first few pages of what is a previously-created 40-page handbook that has been edited to have our school's name and logo in place. Nevertheless, I'm thinking she's only reading the first few pages verbatim and explaining only because it details the first day and first week of school procedures. Much to my chagrin, she literally starts reading each bullet point on every single goddamn page of this handbook! So what should have been maybe 30 minutes of reviewing procedures, unthinkably turns into nearly two hours of unnecessary torture and frustration of just sitting in the auditorium. Halfway into this school year more episodes occurred. One episode would be when administrators make their rounds and visits periodically throughout the year. These visits can be beneficial to administrators to see teachers in action, or perhaps a hidden agenda with the "I gotcha" moment to make an example out of a teacher. A teacher in the social studies department had a surprise visit from the principal with less than five minutes before the bell rang for lunch for everyone. She asks him, "Why aren't the students still working? There needs to be bell-to-bell instruction." Like seriously, what could you possibly be expecting? Teachers and students are ready for a 40-minute lunch break after three 90-minute class blocks. Another teacher stated how she came into the classroom and asked, "Why are the students charging their phones?" I'm sorry, I did not know that you paid the electric bill for the school. Today, cellphones are obviously something that teachers must manage in their classrooms that best fits them. Students unfortunately must use their cellphones in classes to do work or research articles or documents from the Internet because our school does not have enough laptops/tablets for the entire student body. But there are brand new Promethean boards and a large screen TV in the lobby of the school. But with the issue of cellphones, I choose not to fight students over this because it is a battle I am not willing to fight. I just simply swapped out the electrical outlet plates for blank ones in the classroom. As I tell students, you can use your cell phone most of the class, but you will not be able to charge it though, the choice is yours. A second episode of micromanagement would be having an emergency faculty meeting the week after a regularly scheduled faculty meeting. This really was no emergency whatsoever; it was simply a principal wanting to waste everyone's precious time to go over results of an instructional review. An instructional review is when district and regional bigwigs visit to review how teacher-led instruction is taking place in the classroom according to the curriculum, and especially if it is an accountability course. It is the one day when just about every teacher dresses up and has students overly prepared for visitors. Then there is debriefing afterwards between administrators and academic coaches of the school and the district/regional personnel. The findings are then usually disseminated to the faculty either through an email or at the next scheduled faculty meeting. However, we have this 30-minute emergency meeting the same day of this instructional review where the principal is simply micromanaging the entire process discussing everything big and small that happened. On a podcast episode, I weighed in on how exactly a micromanager would have this meeting to really nitpick and try reaching for the skies, when it really was more detrimental to staff morale rather than uplifting. In all honesty, everything that was discussed should have been sent out in an email. Perhaps the biggest takeaway from this emergency meeting was when the principal started talking about strategies to use in the classroom because during their walkthroughs, they noticed that many teachers were still doing the heavy lifting and not the students. In suggesting strategies that teachers could use in their classroom, she refers to the book, Teach Like A Champion, as a perfect example. *[Refer to Chapter 1]* Most of this meeting did not have my attention until the referencing of that book. Only then is when respect goes out the door with that statement, especially given the rhetoric surrounding that book. But possibly the funniest takeaway from this meeting was the fact that she had all her assistant principals holding anchor charts like pawns as she spoke.

A major episode that had mixed results was the disciplinary action against three students who did grade changes in my gradebook and in a fellow social studies teacher's as well. I noticed these grade changes when signing into my gradebook and saw there were five "administrative" grade changes under a column that should always have a zero there. It was Tuesday,

November 8th, a teacher's workday because it was Election Day 2022. My search did not take long to find two of the three culprits of the grade change because a homework grade was changed from a zero to 95. This stood out because I use a regular 4-point scoring system for grades (4=A, 3=B, 2=C, 1=D, 0=F or Z), so anything higher than four points is tagged with the word "MAX" highlighted in yellow with the grade. Obviously, these students who did this are not very bright. The crazy thing was that these students did the grade changes that Monday (11/7) just 2 ½ hours after I originally put the grades in. Plus, on top of that, it was a shutdown day because of the ACT School Day test. However, it took an extra day to find the other student, especially after asking around the department if they noticed any administrative changes in their gradebook. It was undoubtedly the other 12th grade teacher that spotted grade changes as well for this one student whom we both had. Ironically it was a football player. Now your first thought would be that possibly the head football coach or an administrator would pull this stunt. Nevertheless, it was the students themselves who changed their grades because they were able to access the laptop of the person who serves as gradebook manager and dean of discipline, and head football coach. But when this was brought to administration's attention in an email by the other teacher, the vice principal replied with "we need evidence and names with these allegations"? Allegations? So we're defending this kind of activity now for illegally changing student grades? So once I gathered all the necessary information, including the three students' names and screenshots from the gradebook that shows the changes, I emailed administration and all I received in return was just a simple "thank you" from the vice principal. As I mentioned earlier, one of the culprits is a football player, but the crazy thing was that the young man had a "B" in my class. So why even risk this kind of activity and jeopardize possible college football scholarships? One month later, only the football player was reprimanded with only a five-day indoor suspension. Nothing was done to the other two students. Hooray! for discipline and teaching students the seriousness of this illegal crime. Because it is a crime given that a teacher's gradebook is a legal document that can be used in court. What's even more ironic, the one student who was punished did not even attend all five days of his indoor suspension. But this student is also celebrated at graduation for his achievement for earning the most scholarship money as an athlete. Woo-hoo! So perhaps it is true, football players are treated differently than the rest of the student body. Many students and teachers have already pointed out how certain students can break school rules (uniforms, walk the halls, disrespectful, etc.) and nothing is done to them; but a student who commits a simple, but small infraction is made an example of. Where is the fairness in this? The grade changing scandal is one of those moments where the punishment does not fit the crime. Administration says it was only a Level II offense. In all honesty, if the local newspaper or news stations were made aware and/or the region or district were CC'd on the original emails, perhaps the outcome might have been totally different than this Level II bullshit talk. What is even more ironic is this same situation occurred once again the following year. Administrator leaves the work computer/gradebook access open, and a student decides to change their grades in a few classes. Once again, it does not take long for me to find this student who changed grades. You were marked absent for three assignments that were assigned, and then all the grades were changed from a "Z" to "A"??? Like what?! The punishment: a 5-day outdoor suspension and forfeiting a few graduation tickets since this incident occurred in mid-May 2024. Again…Where is the justice? More importantly, where is the leadership?

Social media has been for the past two-plus decades as one of the best ways to advertise yourself and/or your business. Schools have no doubt tapped into this market as well to showcase and put their best foot forward for students and staff, and the community at-large. However, for all the good that social media can be, it can also be a detriment to the good clause as well. When you have a principal who is so inclined to everything, and I mean *everything* on social media, you start thinking to yourself where is the school's priority? During her first year, any good deed that she did for teachers was posted on Instagram or Facebook. One such example was during "Teacher Appreciation Week", every lunchtime activity was either photographed or live streamed online for all to see. I'm sorry, but not everyone wants to have their face plastered on someone's Facebook, *X* (formerly Twitter) or Instagram page. Just about every school activity (i.e. Club Rush, pep rallies) is live streamed so all can see. At some point, it becomes ridiculous! All of this is simply referred to as getting likes for the "gram". Posting every single conceivable moment to be put on social media with no regard of discretion. Even at the beginning of Year 2, during the opening of school's procedures, and later discussed at a faculty meeting much later in the year, a new initiative was spearheaded to highlight a second school website that people would go to view all positive news and information about the school. But why so much effort and energy in this project? There are more pressing issues at this school than worrying about a secondary school website. The school grade fell from a "B" the year before Mrs. Sacramento arrived to a "C". Let's own that "C" and blast it all over social media. Because all the talk about "we're a 'B' school" was not earned with you ma'am. When visiting other schools to model lessons for Cambridge or attend professional developments on a district level, I get asked by other teachers or administrators, "Is it real?" Meaning, is it real with what's posted on social media. My response to that is in the words of Lionel Richie's song: "*Easy (Like Sunday*

Morning)" or "it's all about the likes!" Most times when she resented the use of social media are when the school is casted in a negative light. Examples being when there was a huge 3-fight brawl that broke out towards the end of lunch in early January 2024. It broke her heart that the image of the school was tarnished because so many students had posted videos and different angles of the fight on social media. She was completely livid and went on a rant the next day during morning announcements. What was so crazy about her announcement was that she told teachers "I'm going to give you a few moments to quiet down your classes before I begin to say something very important." Mrs. Sacramento goes into this drawn-out spiel about students not posting negativity on social media and that it was an embarrassment. No ma'am, what really happened was that your fairytale micromanaged school showed its true colors that day. Other incidents with negative social media impact are the other fights within the school posted online. One such fight, or better yet brawl, was an on-campus fight as soon as school got out and multiple videos showing two parents involved, and all of which led to a shooting two blocks from the school an hour later involving the parents of the parties who were fighting.

Probably the most controversial and, the cherry on top, does not even involve micromanaging and all the other foolery, it deals directly with humanity. One of many controversial matters that has made Mrs. Sacramento seems so disingenuous by the faculty are these attendance directives. Many of these directives were issued with no conversation or referral to the Employee Assistance Program (EAP) beforehand during the first year. Many of these teacher directives are outlandish and petty to begin with, but some cut deep when knowing the situation. One teacher was given an attendance directive because they took extra days off because they were closing on their retirement home in another state. Although the principal was notified and had a conversation with this same teacher before school started. In the spring of 2023, she started having teachers called down into her office to sign attendance directives because they took too many days off...personal days at that. Shortly after the Thanksgiving break during her second year, she once again started up once again, but this time having the teachers sign paperwork for the Employee Assistance Program. Everyone's situation is different especially if there are conversations. But perhaps the most insensitive attendance directives were given to teachers who lost a loved one or had surgery. A staff member had a medical procedure done where shortly after; she wanted them back in the office at work. One teacher had lost her father, and anyone who has lost a parent knows the heartbreak and headaches of grieving and taking care of family affairs during this process. In addition, most school districts give their employees bereavement days. But where it becomes heartless, inconsiderate, unsympathetic, and even cold-blooded is the fact that she issued these teachers an attendance directive because they took more days to grieve after the bereavement period. Another example was when a teacher's oldest child was killed in a car crash on Thanksgiving night. Life obviously is never going to be the same for you after the loss of a child (your first born at that) or a loved one especially during the holidays, especially Thanksgiving itself. Mrs. Sacramento started pressuring this teacher to return to work after the Christmas [Winter] break. Only because this teacher is a union member and well-versed in her rights and teacher's contract, she got the union involved to tell the principal to pump the brakes. So to try and make amends, she sends out an email asking teachers to donate a "sick day" to assist the teacher during this hardship. You then honestly start thinking to yourself what kind of principal is running this school? Like can you truly be that callous when someone is mourning the death of a parent or child? I know the previous three principals would tell the employee to take all the time they needed, hands down. Do not worry about your classes or anything, take care of yourself and family needs. During her first year as principal, she had the passing of three loved ones and literally took a month off because her supervisors told her to and utilized the EAP during her extended time off. So where is the same treatment for a staff member who is in the same position? Although not to poke fun or make light of this situation, a few teachers including myself admittedly stated that she should have an attendance directive waiting on her desk upon her return to work. Evidently humanity and compassion does not flow in the veins of this school's principal. The only thing flowing through her veins is seemingly trying to get social media clout by constantly posting on Instagram, *X* (formerly Twitter) and doing Facebook Live when in-school activities are occurring or athletic success on the football field and basketball court; academics are an afterthought. There was full administration support and social media posts when the football team was marching towards an almost undefeated season but came up short in the championship game itself. There was full administration support and social media posts when the boys' basketball team made the playoffs and marched all the way to winning a state championship. Nevertheless, Mrs. Sacramento even goes so far as to try and come up with ideas or programs that were already in place at the school. So you're really not bringing anything new to the table, you actually walked into a high school that was a gold mine with great programs and activities already in place. Perhaps the best thing that could have happened to show her flaws and unpreparedness was when the longstanding activities director was promoted to assistant principal to another high school. What can you do now that the person who could easily run this school by themself is no longer here? But in general, treat people how you would want to be treated. It's not that hard to just be a damn good human being...period!

Another example of where you feel as though the safety of staff and students is lacking was on Wednesday, February 28, 2024. I had just returned to campus after completing a two-day Cambridge History training. During the third block, about 15 minutes before the bell rings for lunch, there is this weird sound of hearing the A/C fan grinding to a complete halt in the A/C duct. There is an eerily silence, and then suddenly, this feeling of very hot (heated) air and the smell of burnt electrical wiring starts flowing through the A/C ducts into the classroom. Stepping out into the hallways and other teachers are noticing the temperature change and smell entering their classrooms too. Some teachers are calling the main office to no avail, so after about one minute, all teachers on the third floor make a collective decision to have their students evacuate the floor. Administration is then asking why are all these students leaving their classrooms on the third floor before lunch? It's only a few minutes later, one of the administrators can be heard over the school P.A. system screaming to evacuate the main building.

Afterwards, the entire school, not just the main building where this electrical fire occurred, but the entire school has now evacuated almost 10 minutes later. But not at any time was the fire alarm pulled to evacuate the building…NOT ONE TIME!!! Firefighters arrive and have their ladders extended to the roof of the main building. One firefighter asks to speak to the principal and is told that she is sitting in her office. The best idea this administration could come up with is to have students report to their last block classes on the third floor and have teachers open all their windows, take attendance, and then move to the gymnasium; a process that would probably take about 15 minutes to complete because students don't necessarily rush to their last block class after lunch. Common sense would be not to have students come upstairs to the third floor and have teachers evacuate from the floor as well. Why have teachers continually, and then students potentially breath and inhale these harmful toxic fumes/particles that could make breathing difficult and cause severe respiratory issues from that electrical fire? What if someone suffers from asthma or bronchitis? The lack of compassion goes even further when not one administrator even comes up on the floor to investigate or see for themselves. Only one administrator actually did come up to the third floor, although it was not until the next morning. Either way, the next day there were still no immediate plans in place to deal with the relocations of teachers from the floor.

However, if all that was written beforehand does not give you a clear picture of what the past two years have been like, perhaps this is the final dagger. Most school districts have banquets to announce their Teacher of the Year (TOY) and Rookie Teacher of the Year winners during the school year. Prior to Mrs. Sacramento becoming principal, our school had celebrated success in these past 10 years with one teacher winning TOY for the district and being the state TOY runner-up, and the second having been one of the finalists for the district's TOY. The previous three principals (Williamsport, Lexington, Austin) all purchased a table or two for the school and the finalist to attend this event and represent. However, it has become very apparent that Mrs. Sacramento has never had any intentions of purchasing a table for the school out of her budget in her two years as principal. A sour note was that the 2023-

2024 TOY representing our school did not even have a table or a purchased ticket to the banquet. Upon arriving at the venue and having waited almost 45 minutes, our school's TOY was then asked her name, employee number, and email address. When she asked why the fifth degree, she was told so she can be billed for the tickets. As crazy as that sounds, it gets worse! So then she and her husband walk in looking for Table 103…they see Table 100, Table 101, Table 102...hmmm, no Table 103. So they do a simple rewind to make sure they did not pass it; after looking again, no Table 103. A server then confirms that there is no table numbered 103. So not only are you embarrassed and humiliated, but now you have to do a walk of shame exiting the banquet with everyone's eyes looking at you again. So upon leaving and trying to turn a terrible night into something positive, they come to the school to cheer on the boys' basketball team against a rival. Now in all of this you may ask, "Where was the principal during all of this?" Very simple: She's at the basketball game, NOT even at the district's TOY banquet herself.

In closing, it clearly shows that Mrs. Sacramento does not truly care for teachers and other staff. She is known to berate her administrators and teachers in data chats and leadership meetings, writing attendance directives for petty and insensitive reasons, and an OCD micromanager who must control the narrative and environment. Everything is a calculated maneuver that solely benefits her and her alone. She is one who is willing to bury, humiliate, and issue punitive disciplinary actions to make herself all-powerful. A person who also feels threatened by the success, integrity, and true leadership skills of other strong Black women in the building. Mrs. Sacramento is the epitome of a cold-blooded, callous person who should not be selected to become a principal; let alone to lead a high school who is elementary ed (education) certified. But as the saying goes, "it's not what you know, but who you know".

Nevertheless, it has not been all terrible in terms of culture and morale at the school in the last two years. There is still great camaraderie among the veteran teachers who have been there ten years or more, or at least the past five years. There are two lighthearted moments that I do remember from the

2023-2024 school year, and they were the Black History program and Grad Bash. The Black History program which was presented by the Fine Arts Department (Drama, Chorus, Dance, Band, Art and Spoken Word) put on perhaps one of the best performances I could recall seeing in years. I had the opportunity of seeing the second show in which the closing act involved each fine art performing collectively to end the show. The climax of this ending brought out emotions of reminiscing from the days of college where you attended performances and activities with your friends that occurred on the campus yard or during homecoming week. The emotions were so strong that I was overcome with joy, had that school pride once again, and for the first time in three years I was proud to say that I love working at my school.

The second lighthearted moment was the senior class trip to Universal Orlando Resort for Grad Bash. This was my second straight year of being selected to chaperone this event, and I was once again looking forward to the fun and excitement; and more importantly, being able to skip the lines as a chaperone utilizing the Express Pass lanes. However, what was supposed to be an exciting experience became a memorable trip for all the wrong reasons. First, the fifth bus was delayed over an hour before arriving at the school. Therefore, instead of leaving at 1:30 P.M., as scheduled, the buses did not depart until 2:30 P.M. in the middle of school dismissal. Second, the fifth bus that I was a chaperone on suddenly breaks down not even a block from the school. Like literally, the bus comes to a complete halt on the street. After about five minutes of the driver talking to dispatch to get the bus started once again, he gets it working and we're on our way. Oh, so we thought, after traveling probably 1,000 feet down the street, the bus breaks down once again. The driver is once again forced to call both dispatch and another driver to get the bus going. During this whole 15-minute ordeal and no A/C, the bus gets rear-ended by a car. All you see is a car speeding around the bus and making a quick right turn at the light up ahead. Luckily the driver and no students were injured. As the trip continues onward, about one hour from our destination, the first bus breaks down, so now those students and chaperones must split themselves among the other four buses. To say the least, we were two hours late to the event, but all the students still had fun considering everything that happened. As if things could not get any worse, the fifth bus once again starts the whole shutting down issue once more at 2:30 A.M. in the morning in the back parking lot of Universal. Luckily, all buses returned back to the school with no further problems. Thank you, Lord!

But if there ever was a way to conclude the previous ten years and the past two years of the current administration would be the handling of graduation 2024. It has been commonplace that if you were not helping with the graduation ceremony, you would take a personal day off to attend the ceremony. A commonplace I have practiced the last couple of years when attending graduation especially since I teach seniors. Call in, have a leave card in place, and go and enjoy graduation and see these young men and women celebrate a major milestone in their young lives. But what is so amazing and mind-blowing about this year is Mrs. Sacramento wants teachers who are attending the graduation but are not helping, to print out this email and attach your leave card and bring it to her; and you will get a ticket based on availability. Like what??? This venue reserves four rows of seating for teachers and staff. But just the audacity and micromanaging of this whole situation. Like you are really that controlling over graduation tickets for the teachers? The ones who put in the work and long hours for 180 days during the school year.

I end this chapter with a quote that I have written on the whiteboard in my classroom, and it states,

"Just because you have a leadership title/role, does not mean you are <u>an</u> <u>effective</u> <u>leader</u>."

Chapter 5

Although this book has discussed the many issues, problems, and concerns when it comes to educating Black youths in the classroom. Criticism and accountability can be equally distributed amongst school administrators, inferior teachers, students, and most importantly the parents. Parents must be involved in all conversations concerning the academic success of their child(ren) for there to be a sense of achievement and prosperity in life.

Parents are their child's first teacher.

Given that statement, a child first learns their ABCs and 123s from their parents. Therefore, parents have to assume culpability for their child's academics. As a teacher, it is disheartening and disappointing with the lack of parental support and involvement especially from Black parents. Black parents are more willing to fight for their child(ren) over foolishness and stupidity, but never when it deals with failing grades and disruptive behaviors in the classroom. First example, parents will get more upset with a teacher for taking a student's cell phone or telling them to put it away because they're on it the entire time and not doing classwork, but not because they received an "F3F" on their report card. Second example would be that parents are willing with no qualms to buy their child $200+ sneakers, the newest Apple iPhone, and the latest clothing and non-essential items; but their child is sitting in the classroom with no paper, pens or pencils, notebooks, or other school supplies in their book bags. Now a parent has every right to buy whatever things they want for their child, but at least make sure they are equipped and prepared with school supplies for the year. Third example would be that on Friday nights during the fall, you can easily find throngs of parents at football games cheering on the players, the marching band, and cheerleaders; even at basketball games too. But when it comes to Open House, majority of parents are nowhere to be found; and when it comes to parent conferences, that's even more difficult to have scheduled. In fairness, I am in full agreement of parents being supportive and being the biggest fan of their child(ren) when they participate in extracurricular activities at school, whether it is sports, band, cheering, drama, chorus, magnets/academies, and clubs. Yet phone calls and emails go unanswered by parents when it comes from teachers or the school. It is no secret to teachers that many parents simply just block the school's phone number in an attempt to avoid having both the school and teachers get in contact with them. Many feel as though the administration or teacher(s) are picking on their child. Which on their part is asinine especially if an unfortunate incident or emergency were to occur at the school involving their child. And given today's school climate, is it really a risk you're willing to take with your own child(ren)? Lastly, parents have become the biggest enablers of their child's poor academics especially when getting them to school on time. Many parents seemed to have no worries or concerns about what time they drop their child off to school. Whenever I had a field trip to attend that departed during the 1st class block; I cannot begin to tell you the countless number of parents dropping students off in front of the school between 8:00-8:45 A.M. with breakfast from either McDonald's, Waffle House, Starbucks, or Dunkin' Donuts. Now mind you, school starts at 7:20 A.M., so that means your child has now already missed over half the 90-minute class block. What makes it worse is that the students then come to class expecting *YOU* to let them eat their breakfast in class. I'm sorry, you are not about to come into my classroom to eat that food unless you brought breakfast for everybody. That is why during the first week of school, I always have a "come to Jesus" talk with both my 1st and 2nd period classes letting them know that if you cannot come to my class on time, you need to get with your counselor and get a schedule change ASAP because you will fail my class coming in after 8:00 A.M. every time. I always tell students that if your parents are constantly bringing you late to school that they are doing a disservice to you and are setting you up for failure later in life. Furthermore, if students are always coming late to school, that means they'll be late to work too. But students consistently say that it's a difference because they're getting paid at work, and to that I say, yes, but at some point, maybe a few weeks later or a month or two, you'll fall back into that habit of being late all the time. Therefore, parents must teach their child(ren) how to honor and value being on time regardless of what it is for. The notion of being "fashionably late" is completely unacceptable.

As not to wholly lambast parents for their lack of involvement, some suggestions are being offered and discussed right now. First, parents must become more hands-on and engaging with their child's teachers. In today's public schools, the gradebook is electronic and can be accessed through the parent portal on the school district's app or website at any time, 24/7. Whereas when I was a student in the 1980s and '90s, my mother had to either call the school or go out to the school to get an update on my grades aside from progress [interim] reports and report cards. But with the availability of an electronic gradebook, there is no excuse or rationale as to why a parent does not know their child's academic progress at any given moment. I have a brutal and honest opinion that if your cell phone has Facebook, *X* (formerly Twitter), Instagram, YouTube and the top gaming apps downloaded, there is absolutely no recourse as to why you cannot take five minutes from your social media or gaming time and check-in on your child's academics. No excuse!

Second suggestion would be that parents need to make the time to attend their child's Open House event at the school. I understand that the date and time may not always be conducive to their work schedule. But an attempt needs to be made. I am amazed that students always ask, *"Am I getting extra credit for coming?"* and my response has constantly been a strong and resounding no. Plus, more importantly, your parents should want to meet and get to know who your teachers are for the school year. I truly do believe that school districts should stop having these open house events 3-4 weeks after school starts and hold them beforehand. Most school districts have teachers report to work a week or a few days early to get their classrooms ready and attend meetings before the first day of school. Why not use one of those teacher workdays as an opportunity for parents to come to the school and greet, or Zoom with all of their child's teacher(s) that day? Yes, it would be a little inconvenient being interrupted a few times every hour by parents, but it is a lot better than having school meetings or mandatory professional development workshops to attend. Any and every opportunity should be exhausted to ensure that parents are able to have that engagement with teachers.

Lastly, parents just simply need to get involved in the academics of their child. It's understandable that most students who struggle or perform so poorly in school probably have parents who struggled or dropped out of high school themselves. Understandably, the curriculums for ELA (English Language Arts) and Reading, and especially Math are much more challenging, complex, and demanding than they were decades ago. But parents need to exhaust all opportunities and resources to ensure that their child can be the absolute best academic student that they can be. Encourage them to attend after-school tutoring, Saturday school, winter and spring break camps, or hire a private tutor. Put in the same effort and energy in helping your child as you would when criticizing and discrediting the school system when they are failing. Also remember to not always take information or misinformation your child gives you at face value regarding what is happening at their school. Do your due diligence and call the school yourself, or without any hesitation drive to the school and speak with someone in the main office.

To epitomize the kind of a relationship that needs to take place for student success, Tiffany Dallas states "Parents and teachers have the same goals. We would function much better as fingers of a closed fist instead of in-fighting like crabs in a barrel". Additionally, my podcast episode entitled, *"New School Year: Advice for Parents"* offers guidance and suggestions for parents too.

Chapter 6

Friday, March 13, 2020. The day that public education

came to a full halt and stop in Florida and across the United

States. I remembered receiving a text message from my

department chair that late afternoon while picking up my two

kids at the time from their schools, stating that we were starting

our spring break a week earlier due to this virus called COVID-

19. Besides, who wouldn't want to enjoy a two-week spring

break late in the school year? Yet, who would have thought

because of this virus that schools across the country would not

reopen and finish the 2019-2020 school year in person? But the

true shock was the record number of reported cases and the

increasing number of deaths in the United States and the world.

But as a teacher who teaches 12th graders, it was truly difficult to

see the Class of 2020 not be able to finish their senior year as all

of us remember our senior year. No Grad Bash, no senior prom,

and more importantly, no traditional graduation with the pomp

and circumstances. But the closing of schools showed once

again that teachers can adapt to the constantly changing

landscape in education. All teachers in today's world must be able to utilize both in-person and online teaching. I have always utilized online learning [Edmodo, Nearpod, EverFi and Teams] in my classes so that students can be prepared for education in the 21st Century. So having to transition to an online platform for learning during the 4th quarter was not completely new. My students were already prepared for the unexpected when it came to online learning with lessons and assignments.

Now I understand that many parents/guardians and grandparents struggled during those last few months of the school year because now they had to do the legwork. Everyone's way of life was turned upside down due to the COVID-19 shutdown. Some people were able to work from home and unfortunately, many people were laid off from work, and of course thousands would lose their lives battling this virus. Due to COVID-19, there was this great appreciation for teachers and the national conversation of raising our salaries because now many, if not all parents finally understood what teachers do and go through in the classroom. During my spare time, I would read tweets and articles, or watch YouTube videos, where parents either praised or complained about teachers and home learning. My favorites were parents getting upset with their child(ren) about not doing their work or totally misbehaving and being rude… "well guess what ma'am or sir, that is how your 'little angel' acts in class every day!" The lying, the sleeping in class, always on their cell phone, the back talking, and the rude attitude is what you are now getting a taste of. Behaviors that teachers deal with on an everyday basis with your "perfect little angel" who is not as perfect when you are not present. But more importantly, home or virtual learning became an extended spring break for most students since there was no accountability or real attempt on their part to learn. Many students would log onto Zoom for their classes and simply keep both the camera turned off and the microphone muted.

When the following school year (2020-2021) was getting ready to start, there was the huge debate of should schools open in-person or begin virtually. I understood the arguments from both sides on this debate. Many parents **(1)** don't believe that this virus is real and/or that children are immune from it, **(2)** believe that their child(ren) will learn better in the classroom with a teacher in front of them, or **(3)** just simply want them out of the house because they were going back to work or tired of them eating all the food, raising the electric and water bills, and putting a strain on the Internet data plan, or just being home period. For many teachers, teaching in the classroom in front of students is the joy that makes us come to work every day. However, this notion that teachers were being lazy or "don't want to do their job" is absurd and asinine. There was a real concern about contracting COVID-19 and bringing it home to our spouses, our own children, or our own parents. But because former President Trump and most in his administration did not believe in science [CDC and Coronavirus task force] and take it seriously, it sent a message to all Americans that the importance of face masks, social distancing, and the vaccines were not important. Even though Trump and many within the White House contracted this deadly virus. But even though schools did reopen for in-person teaching, there was still that concern and risk of contracting COVID-19. Many school districts had contracts or letters of understanding (LOU) agreements in place for teachers' health and salary protection if you contracted and/or had to quarantine due to COVID-19.

Multiple districts utilized a hybrid model where some students came back into the building and the remaining students virtual. Students who returned to the classroom had to wear face masks from beginning-to-end (except for lunch), sit socially distanced in the classroom, and complete their assignment(s) on their own electronic device. There were no handouts, no walking around the classroom to assist students or having students come to your desk for help. These measures stayed in place for the entire 2020-2021 school year. I can truly say the atmosphere at work and in the classroom was so different. The comradery amongst teachers, and between teachers and students was so unusually absent. It felt like a prison at times with the teachers serving as the warden in constantly reminding students to wear their face masks. That love and passion that all teachers have about being in the classroom was truly not there during that school year. Plus, I will admit that it was very difficult to teach while wearing a face mask for 7 hours. Especially if the face mask was made of a material that made it difficult to catch your breath while lecturing your students who were physically in the classroom.

As the Pfizer, Moderna, and Johnson & Johnson vaccines became widely available for everyone ages 5 and older throughout 2021, life has started to return to normalcy like it was prior to March 13, 2020. Even with the availability of the vaccines, the 2021-2022 school year began with uncertainty because of the huge surge of COVID-19 cases throughout the United States in the summer of 2021. Many school districts across Florida and the country either opened with face mask mandates for in-person teaching or virtually once again. But as the school year continued into early 2022, face mask mandates that were either mandatory or optional to start the year had ultimately become optional or ended to close out the school year. Whereas the Class of 2020 that had their high school graduation canceled and done virtually, and special television programs airing to honor them; the Class of 2021 had a socially distanced graduation, and the Class of 2022 graduation returning to the normal pomp and circumstances.

As education in the classroom has returned to normalcy for the 2022-2023 school year and beyond. One thing is apparently clear though, that the shutdown of schools and home learning because of the Coronavirus pandemic has severely impacted the learning progress of students across all grade levels. Students' content knowledge of reading and math regressed, their studying habits worsened, and more importantly their social skills declined significantly upon returning to the classrooms. However, disruptive, and behavioral issues have risen with students returning in-person too. There is also this push to be more conscious of students' mental health awareness in the classroom. According to the National Center for Education Statistics (NCES) within the U.S. Department of Education's Institute of Education Sciences (IES) stated, "Seventy percent of public schools reported an increase in the percentage of their students seeking mental health services at school since the start of the COVID-19 pandemic, and roughly three-quarters (76 percent) of schools also reported an increase in staff voicing concerns about their students exhibiting symptoms such as depression, anxiety, and trauma." NCES Commissioner Peggy G. Carr also stated that "The pandemic has taken a clear and significant toll on students' mental health. This snapshot of the pandemic's mental health impact is critical in informing the need for student mental health services." I cannot stress the importance and seriousness the role of mental health for students has taken on. There isn't a day, or better yet a class period, that does not go by without the Trust Counselor or guidance counselor(s) calling my classroom phone requesting a student to "check in on them". Because many students lost one or both of their parents to the Coronavirus or their parents lost their jobs and thus became homeless, or just how regular life events and occurrences were turned upside down due to COVID. But with the same token, the mental health of teachers should also be a priority of school districts and school administrations. There is this notion that teachers are not human…that teachers are not husbands or wives, fathers, or mothers, or just have a life and deal with everyday issues as everyone else in the world. We are NOT robots; we are human beings and that are allowed to live life as everyone else. In my podcast episode, *Mental Health for Teachers*, I provided ideas and suggestions for how teachers can take better care of themselves mentally. But to drive this point home even further, on a mandatory professional development day (Election Day 2022), I attended a workshop called Youth Mental Health First Aid Training that was very good and informative. Mainly the two instructors taught us how to recognize the signs of mental breakdowns and even suicidal thoughts of students, but that we were only to apply the beginnings of first aid to that student until the proper help arrives. But a co-worker brought up a very good statement about what happens when it comes to mental health and getting help for teachers. He pointed out the fact that a student can get mental services rendered to them by simply asking or being referred, but for a teacher to get mental health services, a teacher has to call the district employee assistance line and have someone there decide whether or not you need to be referred for mental health services. Once again, it illustrates and highlights the importance of teachers' mental health too. A "mental health day" is very important for teachers to utilize those days to simply rest or recharge their batteries, or just their sanctity too. School districts, as well as administration, need to prioritize the mental health of teachers the same as students. Take care of your teachers and we will be there for our students and prepare them to be productive citizens of the world.

Works Cited

Bryant, J. (2015, February 10). Teach for America's truth problem: TFA advocates aren't being honest about education reform, their own agenda. *Salon.* http://www.salon.com/2015/02/10/teach_for_americas_truth_problem_tfa_advocates_arent_being_honest_about_education_reform_their_own_agenda/

Craig, S. (2022, September 11). If you want to do right by students, reconsider Teach for America. *The Georgetown Voice.*

Forman, T. (2020, June). Don't Teach Like A Champion: Reflect, Learn, & Be an Anti-Racist Teacher. Tanesha B Forman. https://taneshabforman.com/2020/06/dont-teach-like-a-champion-reflect-learn-be-anti-racist/

Lemov, D. (2010). Teach Like A Champion. Hoboken, NJ: Jossey-Bass.

Levy, R. (2011, May 28). Teach For America: From Service

Group to Industry. All Things Education.

http://allthingsedu.blogspot.com/2011/05/teach-for-

america-from-service-group-to.html

Moncur, Lemuel R. (Host). (2022, February 6). *Mental Health for*

Teachers [Audio podcast]. Retrieved from

https://raytalkslive.buzzsprout.com/1578562/10019656-

mental-health-for-teachers

Moncur, Lemuel R. (Host). (2022, October 17).

Micromanagement in Education [Audio podcast].

Retrieved from

https://raytalkslive.buzzsprout.com/1578562/11518748-

micromanagement-in-education

Moncur, Lemuel R. (Host). (2021, August 7). *New School Year: Advice for Parents* [Audio podcast]. Retrieved from https://raytalkslive.buzzsprout.com/1578562/8991401-new-school-year-advice-for-parents

National Center for Education Statistics. (2022). *Roughly Half of Public Schools Report That They Can Effectively Provide Mental Health Services to All Students in Need.* https://nces.ed.gov/whatsnew/press_releases/05_31_2022_2.asp

Salazar, R. (2011, September 5). This School Year, Don't Teach Like A Champion. School Leadership 2.0. https://schoolleadership20.com/profiles/blogs/this-school-year-don-t-teach-like-a-champion-by-ray-salazar

Strauss, V. (2017, August 4). Like it or not, Betsy DeVos has

    made a mark in six months as education secretary.

    The Washington Post. Retrieved from

        https://www.washingtonpost.com/news/answer-

        sheet/wp/2017/08/04/like-it-or-not-betsy-devos-has-

        made-a-mark-in-six-months-as-education-secretary/

Treuhaft-Ali, L. (2017). "The Rich Implications of Everyday

    Things" The Jeanes Teachers and Jim Crow, 1908–1968

    (Unpublished Education Studies capstone). Yale

    University, New Haven, CT

Vasquez Heilig, J. & Jez, S.J. (2014). Teach For America: A

    Return to the Evidence. Boulder, CO: National Education

    Policy Center. Retrieved from

    http://nepc.colorado.edu/publication/teach-for-america-

return

About the Author

Lemuel R. Moncur is an alumnus of Morehouse College, holding a Bachelor of Arts degree in History with a minor in Secondary Education. With an extensive background in education spanning close to two decades, he stands as a staunch proponent of academic advancement. In addition to his role as a high school educator, he has dedicated seven years to serving as a summer camp director and after-school tutor for disadvantaged youth. Committed to his role as a husband and father of three, he further engages with the community through his podcast, *Ray Talks Live*, which delves into contemporary approaches to educating today's youth.

Made in United States
Orlando, FL
12 March 2025

59406968R00079